THE
NEW YORK
METS

A Photographic History

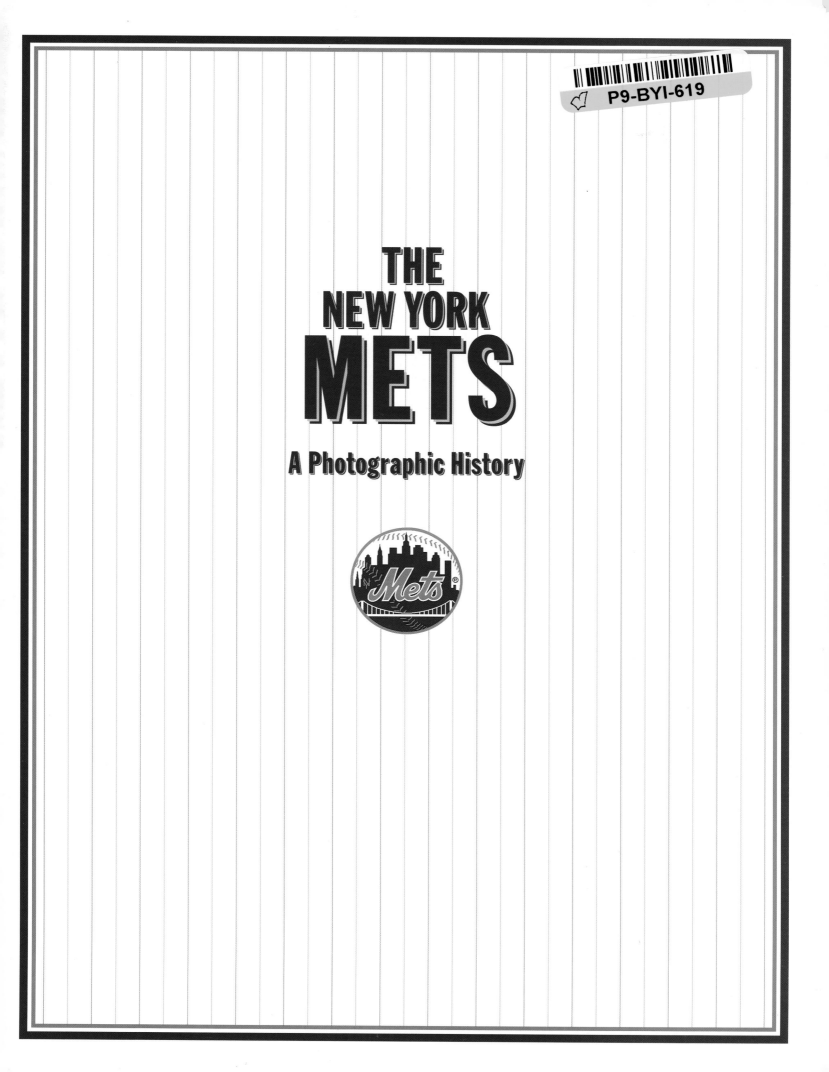

Red Kress

Joe Christopher

Elio Chacon

Red Ruffing

Cliff Cook

Gil Hodges

Chris Cannizzaro

Dave Stillman

Al Jackson

Herb Moran

Galen Cisco

Craig Anderson

Solly Hemus

Jay Hook

Roy McMillan

Bob Kanehl

Jim Marshall

Jim Hickman

Ken MacKenzie

Sammy Taylor

Frank Thomas

Charlie Neal

Marv Throneberry

Bob Moorhead

Casey Stengel

Richie Ashburn

Bill Hunter

Frank Prudenti

Vinegar Bend Mizell

Cookie Lavagetto

JeffWyse

THE
NEW YORK
METS

A Photographic History

Photographs
From the Lens of

George Kalinsky

Special Photographer to the New York Mets
and
Official Photographer of Madison Square Garden

Text by Jon Scher

Design and Art Direction by Robert Engle & Roger Greiner

Macmillan • USA

The editor especially thanks
Robert Engle and Roger Greiner of Robert Engle Design in New York
for their diligence, hard work and incredible effort to get this book completed.
My sincerest appreciation goes to these remarkable professionals.

Macmillan
A Prentice Hall Macmillan Company
15 Columbus Circle
New York, NY 10023

ISBN 0–02–860000–2

Library of Congress data available

Manufactured in the United States of America

10 9 8 7 6 5 4 3 2 1

CONTENTS

ACKNOWLEDGMENTS

I would like to offer my heartfelt thanks to the entire New York Mets organization, to all the players, coaches and club members who have shared their friendship and extended their assistance in so many ways.

First, I would like to express a very special thank you to Fred Wilpon and Nelson Doubleday for always exhibiting support, enthusiasm and loyalty.

Creating this book was a team effort by many skilled and creative people. Mark Bingham of the Mets and Editor Rick Wolff were the leadoff men on this project for having the vision to make this book a reality.

Thanks go to Joe McIlvaine, the Mets Executive Vice President for Baseball Operations, for his friendship and encouragement.

To Mets Media Relations Director Jay Horwitz and his assistant Craig Sanders who contributed their assistance and creativity, as did Dennis D'Agostino, Jim Plummer, Jim Nagourney and Arthur Richman throughout the years. And to Bob Mandt, a Met from day one, who was so kind to open his valuable vault of club memorabilia, and to Daria Amato for photographing it.

To Mets team photographer Marc Levine, who generously made available the club's early photos, and to Louis Requena, the team's first official photographer, who allowed us the use of several of his vintage images. Among the photos in this book are a few by Dennis Burke, who served for two decades as the Mets' staff photographer. Dennis was a consummate professional, and a man whose memory we honor.

My appreciation to Editor Traci Cothran who navigated this project to the finish; to Ken Samelson of Macmillan, the wiz nobody beats; to Betsy Becker for her invaluable research and coordinating; to Robert Engle and Roger Greiner for their beautiful design and commitment to excellence; to Jon Scher for his good words; and to Eileen Miller for artful photo editing.

I am especially grateful to Bill Koras, John Morley, Ed Mazza, Larry Kieran, Mary White, Rich Costa and the Harry M. Stevens family for their support and loyalty throughout my career, and to the Olympus Corporation, whose equipment I've used to record all of these special moments.

To my friend and artist extraordinaire LeRoy Neiman for sketching my portrait that appears on the book jacket, and to Dr. Irving Glick and Herb Schwartzman who inspire me with their special friendship, council and support.

To Marty Appel and Sy Berger of Topps for allowing the use of their Classic Baseball Cards.

For all the joy and loyalty my friends and colleagues at Madison Square Garden have provided.

To the extremely talented George Vecsey of the *New York Times* who is so gentle and caring. Thank you, George, for writing the preface.

And to my wonderful family, who is always there for me—Lee, Ellen Sue, Rachelle, Larry, Fay, Sadye and my wife Ellen, who still makes the sun shine every day.

This page would not be complete without having the honor to thank Governor Mario Cuomo for graciously writing the introduction. From the sandlots of Queens and St. John's University, the Governor engaged in a major league career, rising to become General Manager of the State of New York.

I sincerely thank you all.

George Kalinsky
Port Washington, New York

FOREWORD

Right from the beginning, the Mets were always about humanity. Before they ever played (and lost) a game, there was this appealing aura of mortal hope and mortal frailty.

They were not just a ball team put down in the city of New York to fill seats and sell hot dogs, although surely that is what some of their officials thought they were. The Mets were more than that. They answered some very basic needs for the people who would root for them—the need to care, the need to laugh.

Perhaps more than any other sports team that has ever existed, the Mets were created to replace something. Now think about that. A lot of teams have been plunked down in towns that had never loved and lost before. As North America kept getting bigger, sports teams were slapped up like so many housing subdivisions, and the people went out of curiosity, and maybe eventually came to know something about the game and to create their own mystiques.

But it wasn't raw curiosity that created the New York Mets. It was love and loss. The Mets were specifically based in the National League to replace teams called the Brooklyn Dodgers and the New York Giants who had moved out west after the 1957 season. When the Mets were started in 1962, millions of New York baseball fans already loved them, or wanted to love them, and rather unconditionally, because they were patterned to love a National League baseball team.

So along came these Mets, clumsy and inept, the product of careful, calculating, cunning decisions by other teams. How can we say this gracefully? The players made available by other teams in the expansion draft were not very good. Very few mistakes were made.

Yet the people of New York loved this team. By and large, they loved wrinkled, floppy-eared old Casey Stengel, who was frantically doing a comedian's routine so people would not focus on just how wretched his ball team was. They love Gil Hodges and Clem Labine and Charlie Neal and Don Zimmer and Richie Ashburn and Frank Thomas and Gus Bell and Roger Craig, old National Leaguers trying unsuccessfully to regain their youth. They loved obscure minor-leaguers like Elio Chacon and Rod Kanehl who bumbled so appealingly. They loved the grungy old ball park, the Polo Grounds, where the Giants once had won pennants. They loved Marvelous Marv Throneberry, even when he missed first base on a triple. Or maybe they loved Marvelous Marv Throneberry *because* he missed first base on a triple. They were capable of this kind of love.

This love between fan and team attracted a certain type of journalist and a certain type of photographer. You had to get it, or else maybe you wouldn't go back so frequently. A young photographer named George Kalinsky stumbled upon these New York Mets, and he began snapping pictures of them. George Kalinsky has always been innately drawn to the humanity in people, whether it is Pope John Paul II holding a child in his arms in Madison Square Garden, or the dancer Judith Jamison arranging her angular limbs or the basketball player Earl (the Pearl) Monroe performing the dipsey-doo. George Kalinsky and the New York Mets were a perfect match.

Eventually, the Mets got better, and got worse, and got better, and got worse, much as life does. They won a World Series while the country was shaking as if to come apart in 1969. They won a World Series after Mookie Wilson presided over some peculiar events in and around home plate on a dank Saturday night in October of 1986.

More recently, the Mets fell upon some dismal days, and weeks, and months, and sometimes the fans even stopped coming to the ball park, which fooled nobody, because this is an organization with very deep roots into the hopeful people of the New York region, the people who shrug off disasters big and small and say, "Wait 'til next year"—an old Brooklyn Dodgers saying, you understand.

Through thick and thin, the Mets have always been about the human beings who put on the varied blue-and-orange uniforms, and the human beings who paid their way into the Polo Grounds and Shea Stadium, and the human beings who work there.

There have been some truly great or truly electric heroes on the New York Mets—Managers Casey Stengel and Gil Hodges, young Tom Seaver, old Willie Mays, quick-handed Keith Hernandez, earnest Gary Carter, strong-armed Doc Gooden, powerful Darryl Strawberry.

But what made the Mets truly different, truly special, was the depth of characters—foghorned Looie Kleppel and air-raid-siren-voiced Mother of the Mets, two fans who despised each other but loved the Mets from the far reaches of the Polo Grounds bleachers; hard-working groundskeepers with accents from Ireland and the Deep South; gallant coaches like Joe Pignatano and Bill Robinson; noble third basemen like Ed Charles and Ray Knight who both won World Series and mystically never played for the Mets again; generations of writers and broadcasters and camera operators and photographers.

But most of all, the Mets were the product of the heart and soul of the people who swarmed off the ramp of the Number Seven elevated train, who sat on buses, who navigated ghastly traffic jams on the highways of New York, just to see a baseball team that made them feel. There have been hundreds of great days and nights in the history of the New York Mets (and a few that were not so wonderful). George Kalinsky has been there for many of them. More than a remarkable photographer, Kalinsky is an historian. His work, his pictures, are the bits and pieces of history. In this volume he's opened up his collection of tens of thousands of photographs to share with us the tradition of the Mets, creating for the fans a celebration of the human spirit and a lasting tribute to the human will as seen through the lens of George Kalinsky.

George Vecsey
Sports Columnist
The New York Times

INTRODUCTION

George Kalinsky has spent a career capturing the essence of sports and competition on film. In this, his latest work, his art breathes life into an entire team history.

The story of the New York Mets is one of adversity turned into opportunity. They joined the ranks of professional baseball in 1962 and quickly became a winning entertainment attraction, while losing more games than any team in history. Within seven years the Mets were world champions, repeating their World Series appearance in 1973 and again capturing the title in 1986.

The Mets won the way they began—with spirit and the unwavering devotion of their fans. New Yorkers respect tenacity and perseverance, and the Mets over the years have proved they have plenty of both. We identify with their efforts, and are grateful that George Kalinsky never missed a moment.

Mario M. Cuomo

Mario Cuomo
Governor of the State of New York

From the start, the newborn New York Mets
were colicky and mischievous, troublesome and
difficult—just the sort of team only a
New Yorker could love. During spring training in 1962,
on the eve of that miserable, hilarious first
year, wizened manager Casey Stengel folded his arms
and scanned the flotsam and jetsam on the field.
A crooked smile played across his leathery face.
''If they give us a chance,'' he said,
''we'll steal their underwear.''

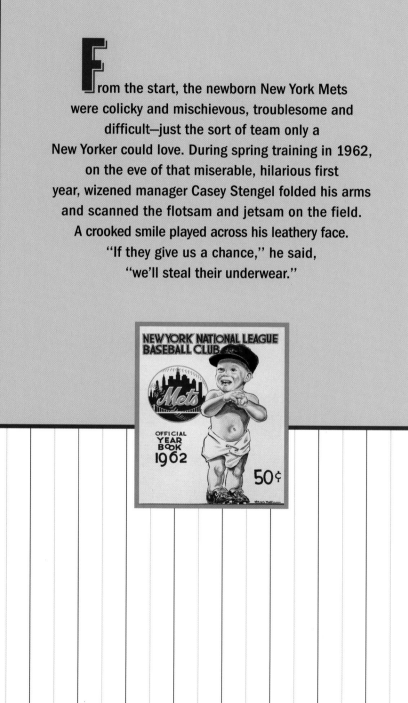

THE AMAZIN' METS

It quickly became clear that the '62 Mets were, ah, amazin.'
They dropped their first game on April 11, losing 11–4 in St. Louis.
Then they came home to New York to the ancient horseshoe
on Coogan's Bluff, just across the Harlem River from
Yankee Stadium. The venerable Polo Grounds had been vacant
since 1958, when the Giants fled to San Francisco.
A crowd of 12,447 braved a steady drizzle
for the opener against the Pittsburgh Pirates, which the
Mets promptly lost 4–3. It was Friday the 13th.

2

1962-1964

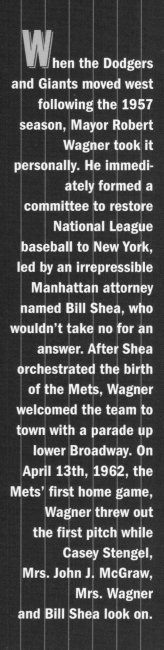

When the Dodgers and Giants moved west following the 1957 season, Mayor Robert Wagner took it personally. He immediately formed a committee to restore National League baseball to New York, led by an irrepressible Manhattan attorney named Bill Shea, who wouldn't take no for an answer. After Shea orchestrated the birth of the Mets, Wagner welcomed the team to town with a parade up lower Broadway. On April 13th, 1962, the Mets' first home game, Wagner threw out the first pitch while Casey Stengel, Mrs. John J. McGraw, Mrs. Wagner and Bill Shea look on.

THE '62 METS

Like guests at their own funeral, members of the 1962 Mets dutifully assembled for an official photo of the worst team money could buy. FOREGROUND: Batboy Harvey Kamnitzer. FRONT ROW, LEFT TO RIGHT: Assistant equipment manager Frank Prudenti, Rod Kanehl, Frank Thomas, coach Red Kress, coach Cookie Lavagetto, manager Casey Stengel, coach Solly Hemus, coach Red Ruffing, Joe Christopher, Gene Woodling, Gil Hodges.

SECOND ROW: Trainer Gus Mauch, traveling secretary Lou Niss, Cliff Cook, Felix Mantilla, Chris Cannizzaro, Richie Ashburn, Al Jackson, Craig Anderson, Ray Daviault, Jim Hickman, Bob Moorhead, Bob ("Righty") Miller, assistant trainer Lynn Lischer, Elio Chacon.
THIRD ROW: Marvelous Marv Throneberry, Sam Taylor, Bill Hunter, Roger Craig, Charlie Neal, Dave Hillman, Vinegar Bend Mizell, Jay Hook, Ken MacKenzie, equipment manager Herb Norman.

THE POLO GROUNDS

For the fans, it was love at first sight. By the middle of their first season, the Mets were packing 'em in at the Polo Grounds. During one five-day stretch they drew nearly 200,000. Sure, the games were against the Dodgers and Giants, but so what? Most people were there to root for the Mets, but even when the home team failed to win, it wasn't exactly a shame. Roger Angell wrote in *The New Yorker,* "This was a new recognition that perfection is admirable but a trifle inhuman, that a stumbling kind of semi-success can be so much more warming."

CASEY STENGEL

I'VE LOVED THE METS ALL OF MY LIFE

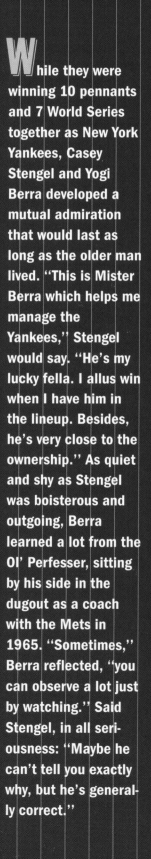

While they were winning 10 pennants and 7 World Series together as New York Yankees, Casey Stengel and Yogi Berra developed a mutual admiration that would last as long as the older man lived. "This is Mister Berra which helps me manage the Yankees," Stengel would say. "He's my lucky fella. I allus win when I have him in the lineup. Besides, he's very close to the ownership." As quiet and shy as Stengel was boisterous and outgoing, Berra learned a lot from the Ol' Perfesser, sitting by his side in the dugout as a coach with the Mets in 1965. "Sometimes," Berra reflected, "you can observe a lot just by watching." Said Stengel, in all seriousness: "Maybe he can't tell you exactly why, but he's generally correct."

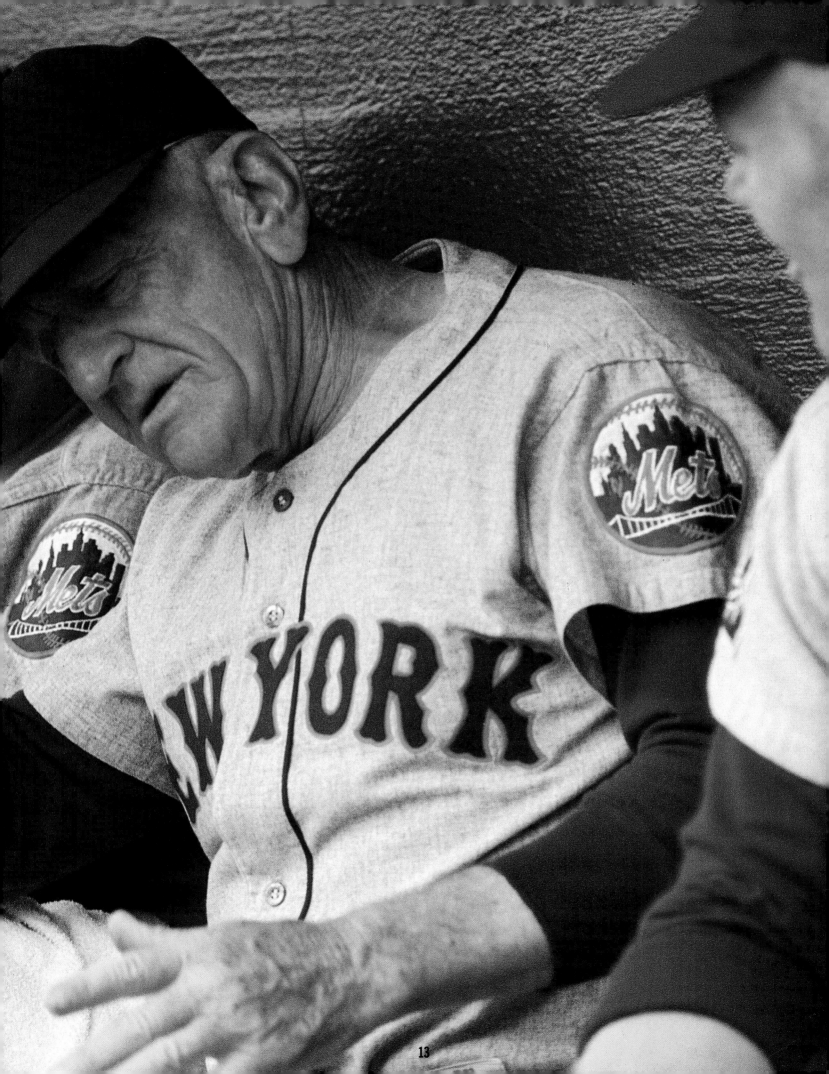

Stengel loved an audience, and the writers who covered the Mets in their dreadful early years were happy to oblige. No one could possibly provide better copy. "The Mets," Stengel promised in spring training, "are gonna be amazin'!" After games at the Polo Grounds, the writers would surround his desk in John McGraw's old office, to watch him smoke, chug a beer, and offer colorful ruminations. "I was the best manager I ever saw," he once said, "and I tell people that to shut them right up, and also because I believed it."

The Mets moved into Shea Stadium in 1964, a year behind schedule. "Lovely, just lovely," Stengel mused, "a lot lovelier than my team." Before the opener, Guy Lombardo and his Royal Canadians were ensconced on the outfield turf, in front of walls that were still being painted. Stengel, of course, couldn't resist taking a turn as the leader of the band. "When you're young," the old man said before a 4-3 loss to the Pirates, "it's great to go into a stadium where your future lies in front of you."

After he fell and broke his hip at a party at Toots Shor's restaurant in the middle of the '65 season, Stengel was done with managing. But not with the Mets, who named him a vice-president without portfolio and brought him back for every special occasion, including, of course, Old Timers' Day.

CASEY
STENGEL
N. Y. METS   MGR.

DUKE
SNIDER
NEW YORK METS   OF

METS

RON HUNT   2nd base

ROGER
CRAIG
N. Y. METS   PITCHER

GENE
WOODLING
NEW YORK METS   OF

GIL
HODGES
N. Y. METS   1B

CRAIG
ANDERSON
NEW YORK METS   PITCHER

FRANK
THOMAS
NEW YORK METS   OF

JOE
CHRISTOPHER
N. Y. METS   OF

Can't anybody here play this game? Stengel with Sammy Taylor, Dave Hillman and Harry Chiti.

He couldn't run. He couldn't field. He couldn't throw. Once in a while, he would hit for power. But Marv Throneberry wasn't a typical one-tool player. His failures were nothing less than spectacular. On a triple, he once forgot to touch first *and* second base. The press quickly dubbed him Marvelous Marv, and he became a cult hero, a symbol for the marvelously inept Mets. Fans would chant his name and bring banners to the Polo Grounds celebrating his marvelousness. One banner read, CRANBERRY, STRAWBERRY, WE LOVE THRONEBERRY.'

MARV
THRONEBERRY
NEW YORK METS
1B

Marv Throneberry, Richie Ashburn and Frank Thomas

Marvelous Marv actually had the best year of his major league career for the '62 Mets, hitting .244 with 16 homers. But that was lost in all the commotion about his celebrated blunders. Somehow, Throneberry bore the notoriety with humor and grace. In appreciation, New York baseball writers gave him the Good Guy award at their post-season dinner. "They told me not to stand up here too long holding the plaque," he said. "I might drop it."

THE YOUTH OF AMERICA

Commissioned in 1965 by Mets owner Joan Payson, sculptor Rhoda Sherbell produced a bronze statue of Stengel that is, to be sure, an amazin' likeness. The assignment wasn't easy. When Sherbell met Stengel before a game at Shea and told him what she was planning to do, the old manager had an unusual reaction. "He asked me how I would like him to pose, and went into a little dance right there," Sherbell said. "He was doing pirouettes, and the crowd was cheering, but I had to tell him that was not what I needed. I sketched him the best I could, but I finally had to work from pictures." Sherbell's masterpiece, a magnet for kids, is in the permanent collection of the Queens Museum.

1964-1968

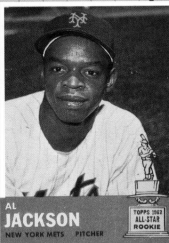

AL
JACKSON
NEW YORK METS   PITCHER

TOPPS 1962
ALL-STAR
ROOKIE

Casey Stengel loved Al Jackson. According to Stengel's biographer, Robert W. Creamer, Stengel thought Jackson "a fine pitcher who could field his position skillfully, handle a bat well, run bases intelligently, and pitch with guile and courage." Said Jackson, who twice went 8–20 for the Mets, "He never treated me with anything but respect." Stengel would cock his head and wink when Jackson's name came up. "A *pret*-ty good-looking pitcher," the Ol' Perfesser would say.

AL JACKSON

CHOO CHOO
COLEMAN CATCHER
N. Y. METS

Early in the '62 season, Ralph Kiner invited catcher Clarence (Choo-Choo) Coleman on his post-game show. "Choo-Choo," Kiner said, "could you tell us how you got your nickname?" Coleman said he didn't know. "Well," Kiner bravely went on, "what's your wife's name, and what's she like?" "Her name's Mrs. Coleman, and she likes me," replied Choo-Choo. Coleman's time in New York was all too brief. "Choo-Choo would give you the sign and then look down to see what it was," remembered pitcher Roger Craig.

BEHIND THE SCENES

The very first time George Kalinsky carried his camera into a major league locker room, he came face to face with one of his heroes. It was Old-Timers' Day at Shea in 1965, and Jackie Robinson (far right) was signing balls along with Don Newcombe, whose son waited patiently. "I always admired Robinson for his fierceness and competitiveness," Kalinsky says today. "But when I saw him up close, I noticed a deep sadness in his face. It was as though what he had gone through as a human being had left a lot of tarnish on his soul. I remember feeling sorry for him because of that."

WARREN SPAHN

Who was this old coot with the thinning hair and prominent beak? Could it possibly be Warren Spahn—the great Warren Spahn? Sadly, it was. After a lifetime with the Braves, Spahn—or, rather, his remains—came to the Mets and went 4–12 before moving on. Spahn was bemused by the reunion with Casey Stengel, who had managed him as a rookie with the 1942 Boston Braves. "I played for Stengel before and after he was a genius," Spahn joked.

Tug McGraw struck out the first major league hitter he faced, Orlando Cepeda of the Giants, then danced a jig on the mound. In his second start, on August 26, 1965, the 20-year-old McGraw became the first Met to beat Sandy Koufax. The Dodger ace, on his way to the Cy Young Award, had won 13 in a row against the Mets. McGraw was awestruck. "The night before," he said. "I just tossed and turned. I kept thinking of Koufax."

Afterward, Koufax was thinking of McGraw. "Good fastball," Koufax remarked, paying the rookie a supreme compliment.

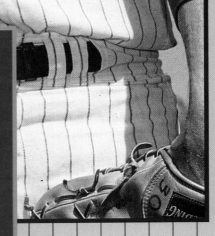

Despite all the attention he received because of his obvious talent, Nolan Ryan never aspired to be in the limelight. He really wanted to be a veterinarian. "My goal," he later said, "was to get four years in to qualify for the pension. Then I'd go to work." That, to him, was much more appealing that being subjected to a barrage of questions from the likes of Howard Cosell, who always seemed to be around.

"It was all a little overwhelming," Ryan said, "and it wasn't fun."

When Lynn Nolan Ryan was 11 years old, he gashed three fingers and sliced the tip off his right thumb while trying to remove the jagged top of a coffee can. Scar tissue formed, and pitching caused calluses to build. Underneath the calluses, painful blisters would erupt. Nothing seemed to prevent the problem, which continually landed the hard-throwing Ryan on the disabled list. Mets trainer Gus Mauch knew that pickle brine had been used to toughen the feet of boxers in training. Wondering if it might do the same for Ryan's fingers, he went to a corner deli and picked up a jar. For weeks, Ryan would soak his fingers in the brine, gamely posing for photographers. Needless to say, the treatment was ineffective. But it was great for the deli, which posted a sign in the front window: "Nolan Ryan Buys His Pickle Brine Here."

NOLAN RYAN

33

TOM SEAVER

DONN CLENDENON

GIL HODGES

Casey Stengel may have made the Mets Amazin', but Gil Hodges made them champions. Even those who felt Hodges' wrath, who withered in his icy glare, harbored respect for the man. "The key to it all," said Cleon Jones, who was once yanked from left field because the manager thought he lacked hustle, "was Gil Hodges." As a leader, he was demanding, but fair. "It's the only way to operate," he said. "You must treat them all as men."

35

Sportswriter Dick Young called Jerry Koosman "a cool cat," because, like Warren Spahn, he would sit on the bench in the dugout on days he was pitching and joke with reporters and teammates. Koosman's confidence, in himself and the Mets, was unshakeable. "No matter who is up there at the plate," said reliever Ron Taylor, "Kooz believes he can get him out." Most of the time, he was right. Koosman won two World Series games in 1969, including the clincher. "We're happy," he said, "but we've been happy all year. It isn't a strange idea to us that we should win. We really think we should." In 1978, when he was traded to the Twins for Greg Field and a player to be named later— who turned out to be Jesse Orosco, the reliever who was on the mound when the Mets won in '86—he spoke with Joseph Durso about the '69 miracle. "Before I pitched the final game," Koosman said, "Pearl Bailey was talking to me and she said, 'Don't worry, I know you're going to win. The only thing I don't know is the score. But I see a number 8.' The final score was 5-3. She had that ESP."

JERRY KOOSMAN

RON SWOBODA

He'll always be remembered for the tremendous backhanded
diving catch he made on Brooks Robinson's ninth-inning drive to save Game 4 of the World Series,
but muscular right fielder Ron Swoboda won more than a few for the '69 Mets.
Swoboda was one of the men who made the Miracle. "The way we're going," he told Larry Merchant
in September, "it's hard to keep your feet on the ground. You feel inebriated, high.
If they could package us, I don't think we'd be legal."

Tom Terrific had the unerring ability to keep things in perspective. "If you want to know what I would like to do," Seaver told Dick Schaap late in his career, "I would like to be a great artist. I would like to be a great painter. I would quit pitching right now if I could paint like Monet or Rousseau or Pissarro. But I can't. I wish I could, but I can't. What I can do is pitch a baseball, and I can do that very well."

Hard-throwing rookie Gary Gentry started the third game of the World Series against the Baltimore Orioles at Shea Stadium. Although Gentry hadn't given up a run, when he walked the bases loaded with two outs in the seventh inning, manager Gil Hodges ran out of patience. Hodges lifted Gentry and brought in Nolan Ryan, who saved the game that put the Mets ahead in the Series. On his way to the dugout, Gentry basked in the cheers of the fans.

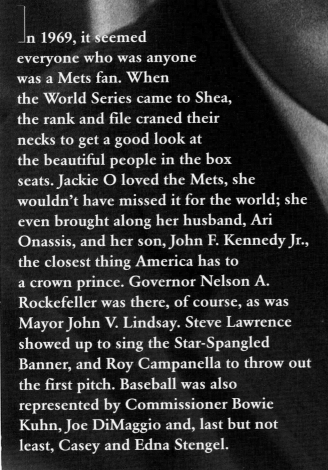

In 1969, it seemed everyone who was anyone was a Mets fan. When the World Series came to Shea, the rank and file craned their necks to get a good look at the beautiful people in the box seats. Jackie O loved the Mets, she wouldn't have missed it for the world; she even brought along her husband, Ari Onassis, and her son, John F. Kennedy Jr., the closest thing America has to a crown prince. Governor Nelson A. Rockefeller was there, of course, as was Mayor John V. Lindsay. Steve Lawrence showed up to sing the Star-Spangled Banner, and Roy Campanella to throw out the first pitch. Baseball was also represented by Commissioner Bowie Kuhn, Joe DiMaggio and, last but not least, Casey and Edna Stengel.

AL WEIS

It may have been the biggest Miracle of all. Al Weis,
the Mets' journeyman second baseman,
hit six home runs in his first seven major league seasons. When he took
Dave McNally deep to tie the score in Game 5 of the World Series, Weis wasn't sure what to do.
So he put his head down and ran for his life, slowing down only after he
reached second base and registered the roar of the crowd. "Was I shocked?" asked Weis,
a career .219 hitter who batted
.455 in the Series. "Hell, yes!" Not half as shocked as the Orioles.

THE CATCH

396

With two outs and the bases loaded in the top of the seventh in Game 3 of the 1969 World Series, Baltimore's Paul Blair hit a slashing liner into the gap in deepest right-center field.

"If the ball drops," Blair thought to himself as he neared second base, "I might have an inside-the-park home run." That would have trimmed the Mets' 5-0 lead to a whisker. Instead, the side was retired in spectacular fashion, when center fielder Tommie Agee raced for the ball, tapped his glove, then made his famous diving catch. It was Agee's second sensational play of the game. Three innings earlier, he robbed Elrod Hendricks of an extra-base hit with a backhanded catch, saving two runs.

"Do you believe the Mets are a team of destiny?" Orioles manager Earl Weaver was asked.

"No," he replied. "I believe the Mets are a team with some fine defensive outfielders."

THE FINAL OUT

Before the World Series opened in Baltimore, Cleon Jones arranged for a brand-new TV to be delivered to the Mobile, Alabama, home of his grandmother, Myrtle Henderson. So Mrs. Henderson, who raised him, was able to enjoy the greatest moment of her grandson's life in living color. With the Mets leading 5-3 and two outs in the top of the ninth in Game 5, second baseman Davey Johnson hit a Jerry Koosman pitch to deepest left-center. Jones camped under it. "Keep dropping down to me, baby," he said to the ball. "Keep dropping down." He extended his hands to make the catch, and he and Tommie Agee, his old high school football teammate, began racing for the bullpen in right field. In the clubhouse, Jones was jubilant. "Some people still might not believe in us," he said. "But then, some people still think the world is flat." As for Mrs. Henderson, she believed.

WORLD CHAMPIONS

It was another turbulent year in America, full of fabulous highs and terrible lows. Nixon was in the White House. Young men were dying in Vietnam, while antiwar sentiment at home was growing more intense every day. Men walked on the moon. Hundreds of thousands gathered in a field near Woodstock, in upstate New York, to celebrate three days of peace and music. Then, at 3:17 p.m. on October 16, 1969, the Mets won the World Series, bringing a joyful noise to New York City. For a few fleeting moments, hope triumphed over cynicism.

With a tremendous roar, the human wave rose from the stands and crashed onto the field. It was riotous, it was frightening, it was too wonderful to describe. It was like V-E Day, the Fourth of July and New Year's Eve all rolled into one. The New York Mets were the champions of the world, and, on this day at least, anything was possible. Tom Seaver could barely be heard over the pandemonium in the clubhouse. "It's beautiful!" he screamed. "Beautiful! Beautiful! Beautiful! It's the biggest thrill in my life! We played to win. We never quit. We'd come from behind to win. We did it today! Beautiful! Beautiful! Beautiful!"

1969 WORLD SERIES
NEW YORK METS

Son of Joseph Agee of Mobile, Alabama, Tommie Agee was overwhelmed by the tumult in the victorious Mets' clubhouse. "I'd almost rather be back in the peace and quiet of ninth place," he joked, ducking into the trainer's room to share a moment of serenity with his proud father.

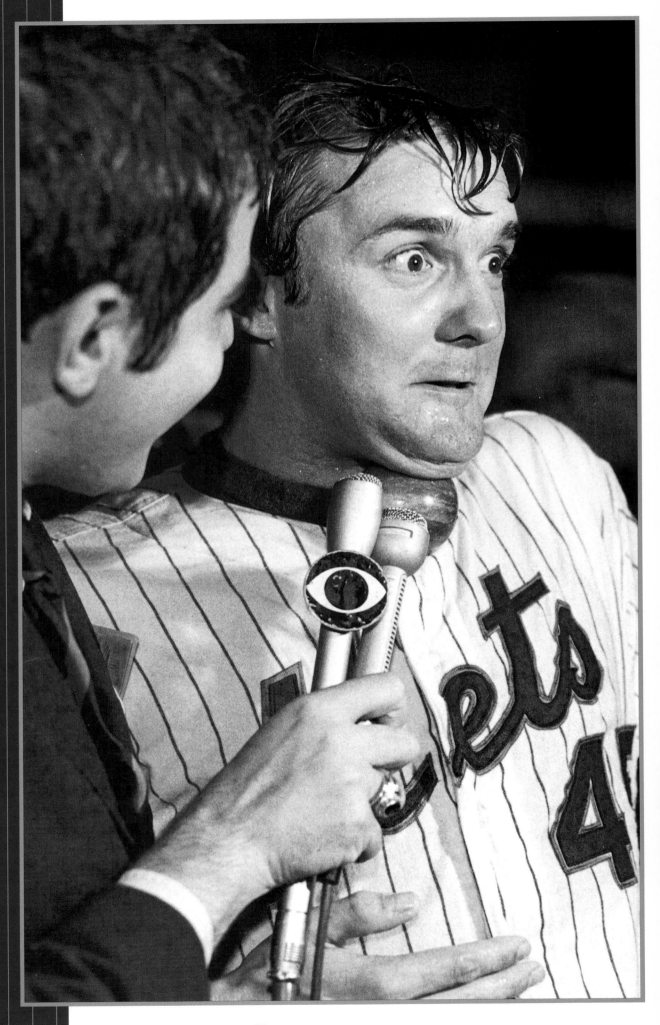

From the time he was born, Frank McGraw set out to enjoy everything life had to offer. His impatience while feeding at his mother's breast led her to nickname him Tug. As the ace of the Mets' bullpen, lefthanded Tug McGraw lent a whiff of whimsy to the Miracle year. "Happy-go-lucky," said Gil Hodges. "A little flighty. Up in the air." In 1969, he never came down. After the World Series, an astonished McGraw used his winner's share to spruce up The Bullpen, the mobile home he shared with his wife, Phyllis, and their dog, Pucchi. "We got a hot water heater and a Porta-Potti," he said with pride. "Now I've got it made."

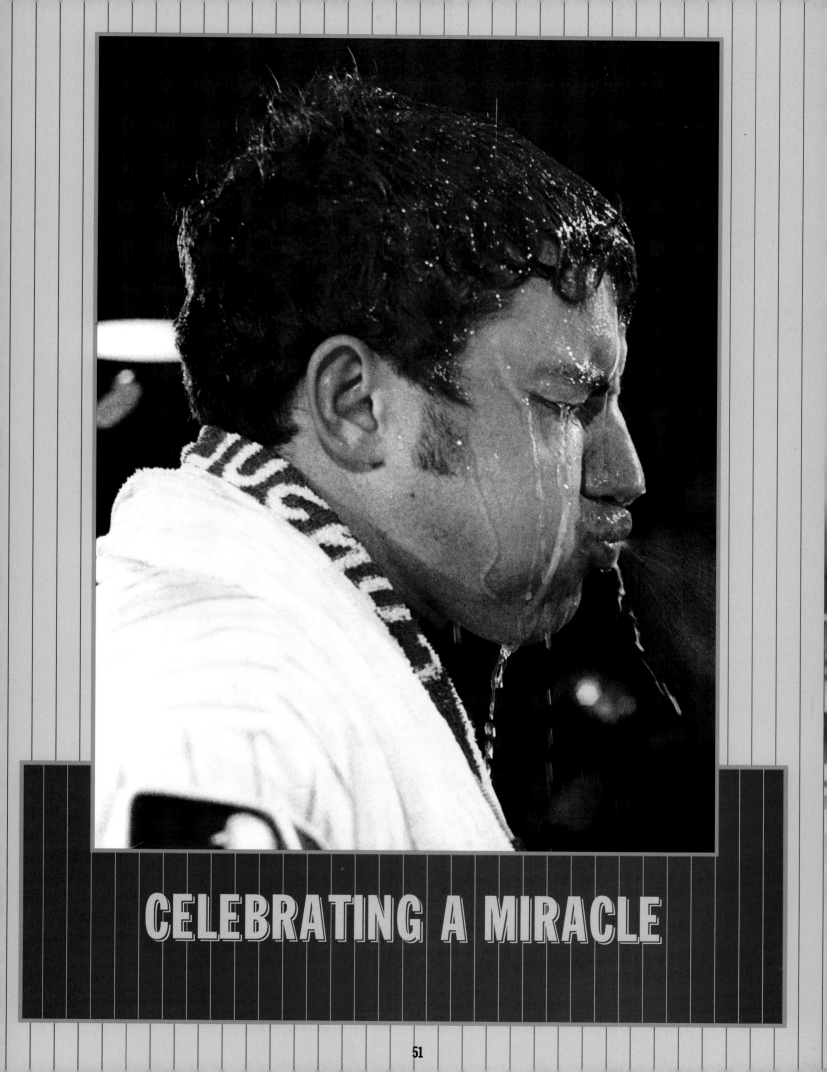

CELEBRATING A MIRACLE

Long before he became the man who ran Tom Seaver out of town, M. Donald Grant was just another rich guy with a free pass to the Mets' clubhouse. In the aftermath of the team's historic World Series victory, Mrs. Payson's personal financial guru communed with regular guys like Tug McGraw and Jerry Grote. "Our team," he gushed, "has finally caught up with our fans."

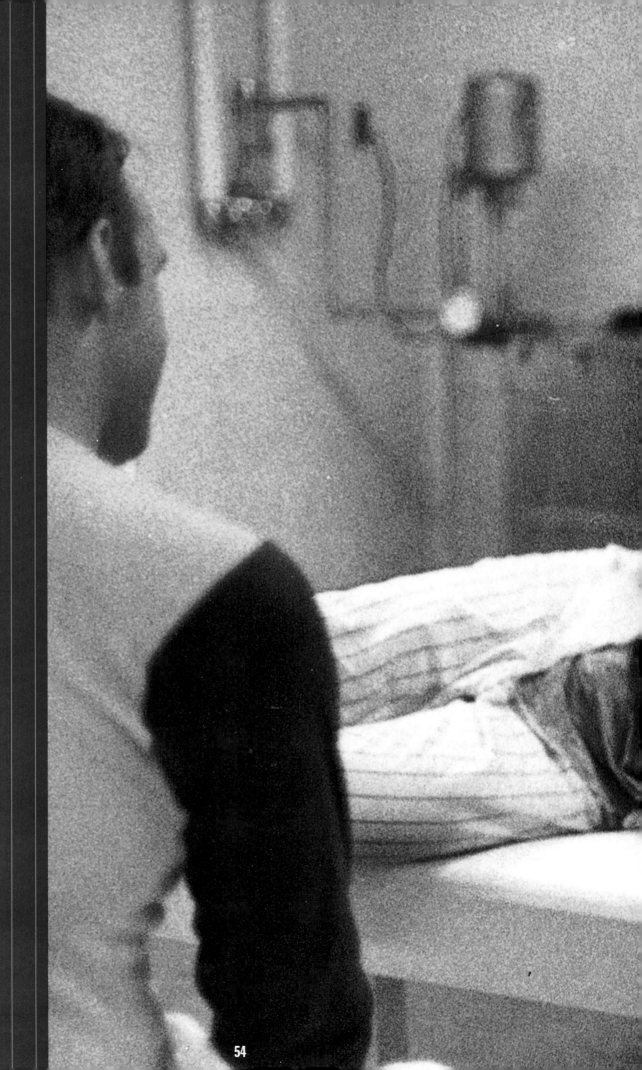

When the crush of media, celebrities and well-wishers in the clubhouse got to be too much, Tom Seaver, Wayne Garrett and a few of the other Mets took refuge in the trainer's room to savor their Miracle. Said Seaver, "It was the greatest collective victory by any team in sports."

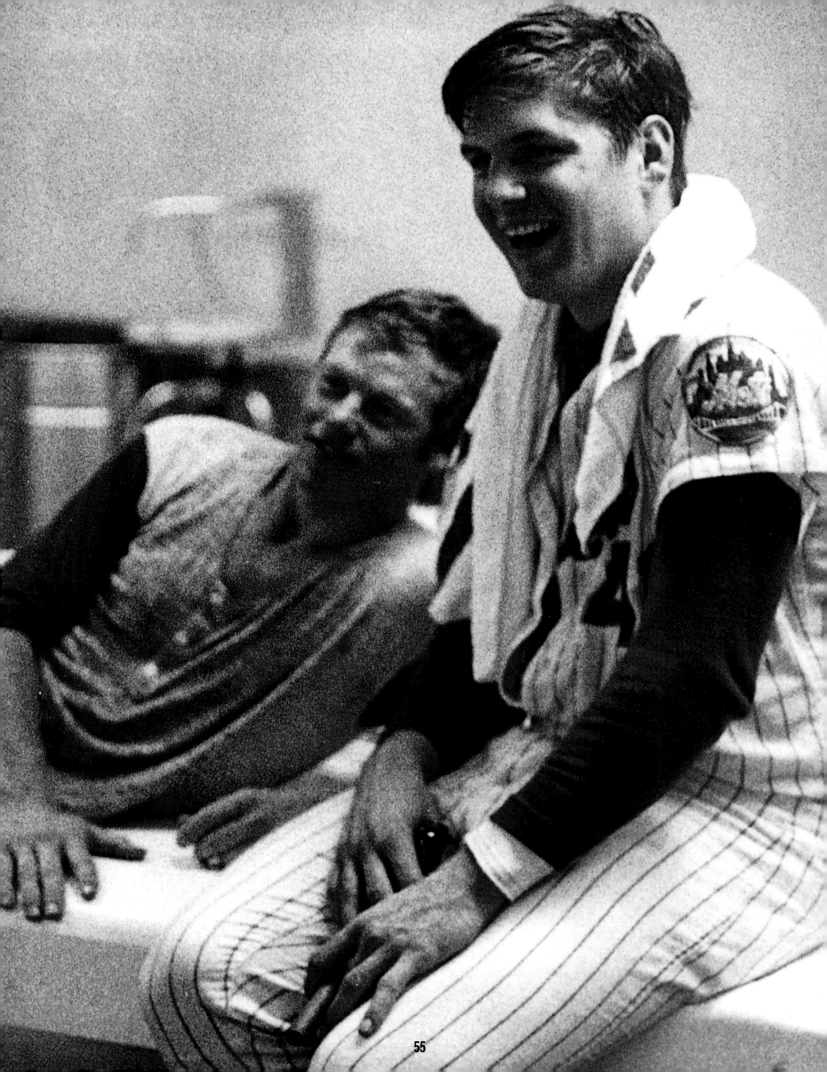

ED CHARLES

One of nine children from a hardscrabble background, Ed Charles spent a decade in the minors. When the World Series was over, so was his career. After waltzing in the clubhouse with Pearl Bailey (above), Charles, 37, took off his uniform for the last time. "My 20 years in the game were wrapped up in that one season," said the Mets' poet laureate and part-time third baseman. "It was a miracle."

Tom Seaver and Gary Gentry returned to the mound during the locker room party hoping to celebrate with some of the loyal fans. As Gentry later recounted to George Kalinsky, they were disappointed to find that the crowd had already dispersed, leaving only the patches of torn-up grass where they'd taken a bit of the memory home with them.

Gil Hodges (at center) was a quiet man, but he celebrated the Mets' World Series triumph in his own way. During the victory parade, he hugged and kissed his wife, Joan, as they rode in a convertible through a blizzard of tickertape on Broadway. In Brooklyn, where he played and lived, he delighted a crowd at Borough Hall by donning an old Dodgers jacket. His home was on Bedford Avenue, not far from the site of Ebbets Field; the thoroughfare was designated Gil Hodges Street in recognition of the Mets' miracle. He always deferred the credit to his players. ''It was a colossal thing they did,'' Hodges said. ''These young men showed that you can realize the most impossible dream of all.''

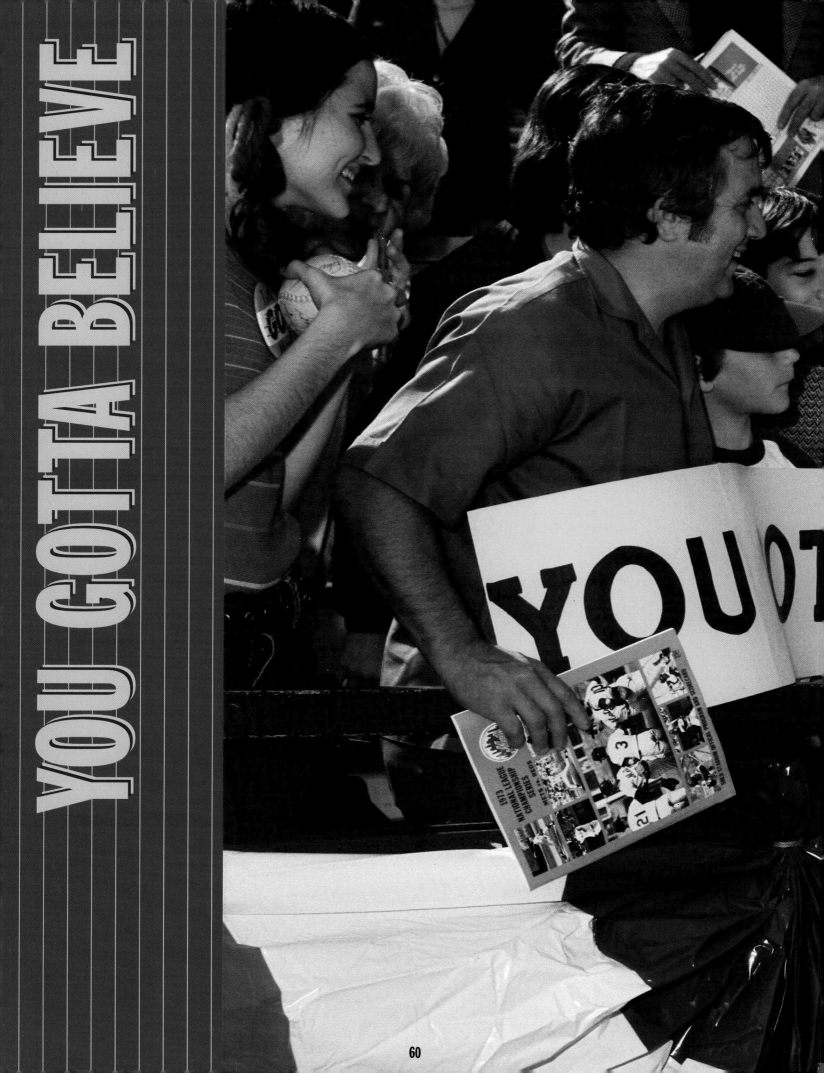

YOU GOTTA BELIEVE

1970-1973

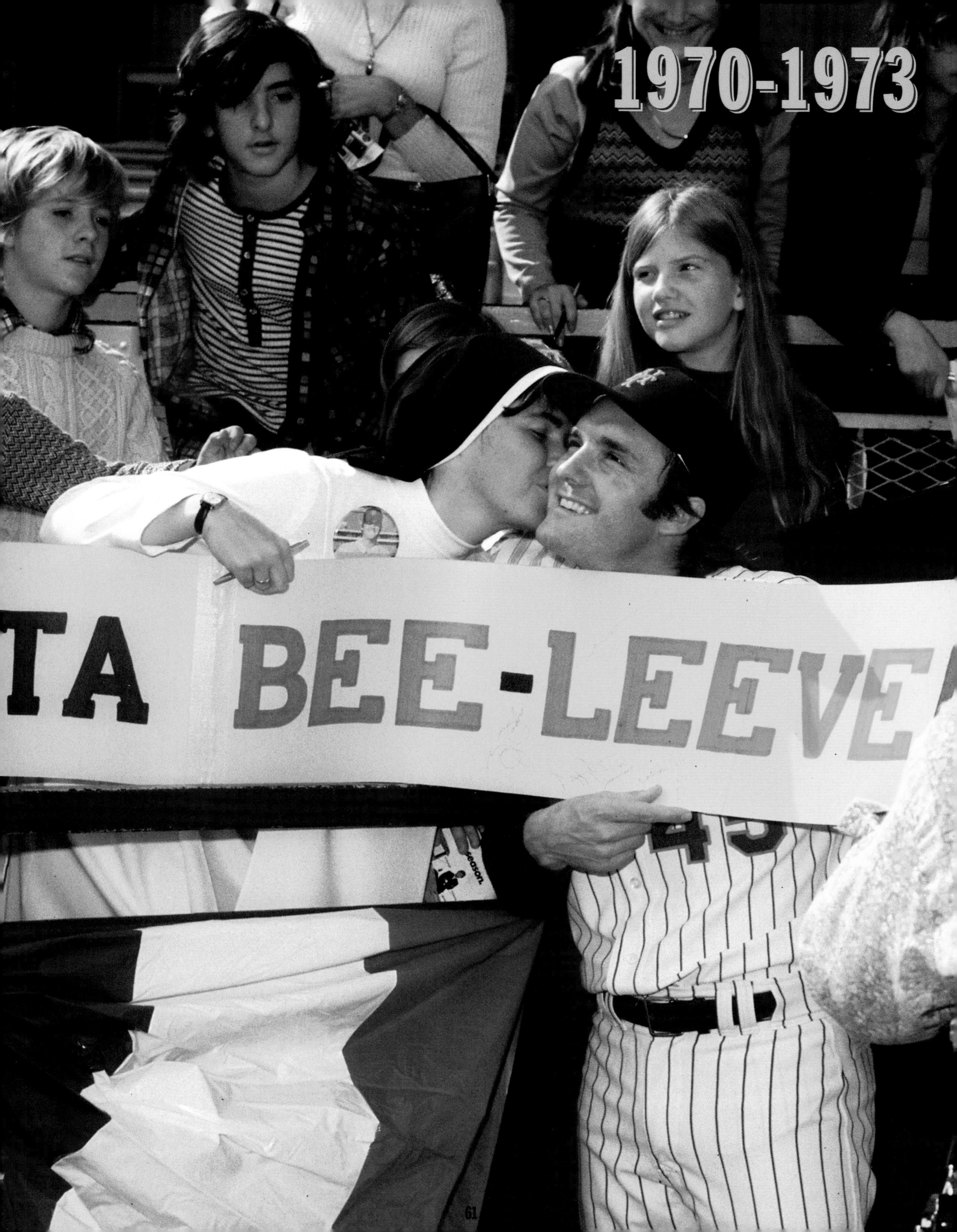

With a vengeance, the Mets rose from last place in the final weeks of the 1973 season. Inspired by reliever Tug McGraw, whose rallying cry was ''You Gotta Believe!,'' they won 29 of 43 to finish 82-79 and capture the NL East crown in a mad scramble. Then they faced the unenviable task of taking on Cincinnati's Big Red Machine in a best-of-5 playoff. The Reds had won the West with a 99-63 record, but the pitching-rich Mets took them apart. Seaver and McGraw combined for a 7-2 win in Game 5 at Shea, and the Mets bathed in champagne.

Two collisions on the base paths during the 1973 season had earned Bud Harrelson a broken wrist and a fractured cheekbone, so when Pete Rose hit him with an elbow to the head while sliding into second base trying to break up a double play in Game 3 of the playoffs, Harrelson was in no mood to say how-do-you-do. "He came into me after I threw the ball," Harrelson said. "I'm not a punching bag. I didn't like what he did, and he didn't like what I did." Harrelson cursed at Rose, and the Reds' burly outfielder pushed the Mets' shortstop. The fight was on.

Both benches and both bullpens emptied, and Rose and Harrelson soon found themselves surrounded by a sea of flailing bodies. It took 15 minutes to restore order, and as the fighting broke up,

Cincinnati relief pitcher Pedro Borbon emerged wearing Buzz Capra's blue Mets cap. When he realized he had it, Borbon took off the cap, bit it, and tore it apart. Later, Rose was unrepentant. "I play hard," he said, "but I don't play dirty. If I was a dirty player, I could have leveled him." Harrelson got the worst of the scuffle. "Fighting is like sex," he said. "It doesn't make any difference whether you're on the bottom or the top. I'm a lover, not a fighter."

In the aftermath of the Rose-Harrelson melee, Reds manager Sparky Anderson pulled his team off the field when fans in the left-field stands pelted Rose with debris. The Mets were threatened with a forfeit, but the tide of anger subsided and the game went on.

In 1973, as player after player went down with injuries, manager Yogi Berra was stoic. He didn't flinch, not even when board chairman M. Donald Grant issued this tepid vote of confidence: "We have no thought of replacing Yogi. We will not do so, unless forced to do so by public opinion." In August, with the Mets in last place, Berra saw a light at the end of the tunnel. "I'm not saying it's going to happen, but it's there," he said. "We can still win. You're not out until you're out." After the Mets beat the Reds for the pennant, setting off another delirious celebration at Shea, he was as ecstatic as Yogi can be. "I never gave up," he said, "and neither did the players."

Rusty Staub would do anything to win—"Whatever it takes," the big redhead would say. In the fourth game of the '73 playoffs, he crashed into the outfield wall while making a spectacular catch, and separated his right shoulder. Despite the nagging injury, Staub hit .423 in the World Series against the Oakland A's.

RUSTY STAUB

JERRY GROTE

Where was no better catcher in baseball. Sure, there were catchers who were better hitters—Johnny Bench, for example—but defensively, no one was better than Jerry Grote. Fiery and cantankerous, Grote was a man you didn't want to cross. When he blocked the plate, it stayed blocked. "He was durable, aggressive and agile," pitcher Jon Matlack said in 1977, after the Mets traded Grote to the Los Angeles Dodgers. "He'd come out from behind the plate so fast that he's beat me to bunts. He could throw like hell, too."

They may have had the lowest winning percentage of any league champion in baseball history, but the 1973 Mets would not be a pushover in the World Series. In fact, they came close to unseating the defending champion Oakland A's, a powerful club in the middle of what would become a colorful three-year reign. Reggie Jackson hit .310 and was named MVP, Rollie Fingers saved two games and allowed one earned run in 13 innings, and the A's triumphed in the last two games at home to win the Series. Second baseman Felix Millan (above) forces out Reggie Jackson and throws to first to complete a double play in Game 2. Millan joined the Mets in 1973 and played a major role in their pennant drive.

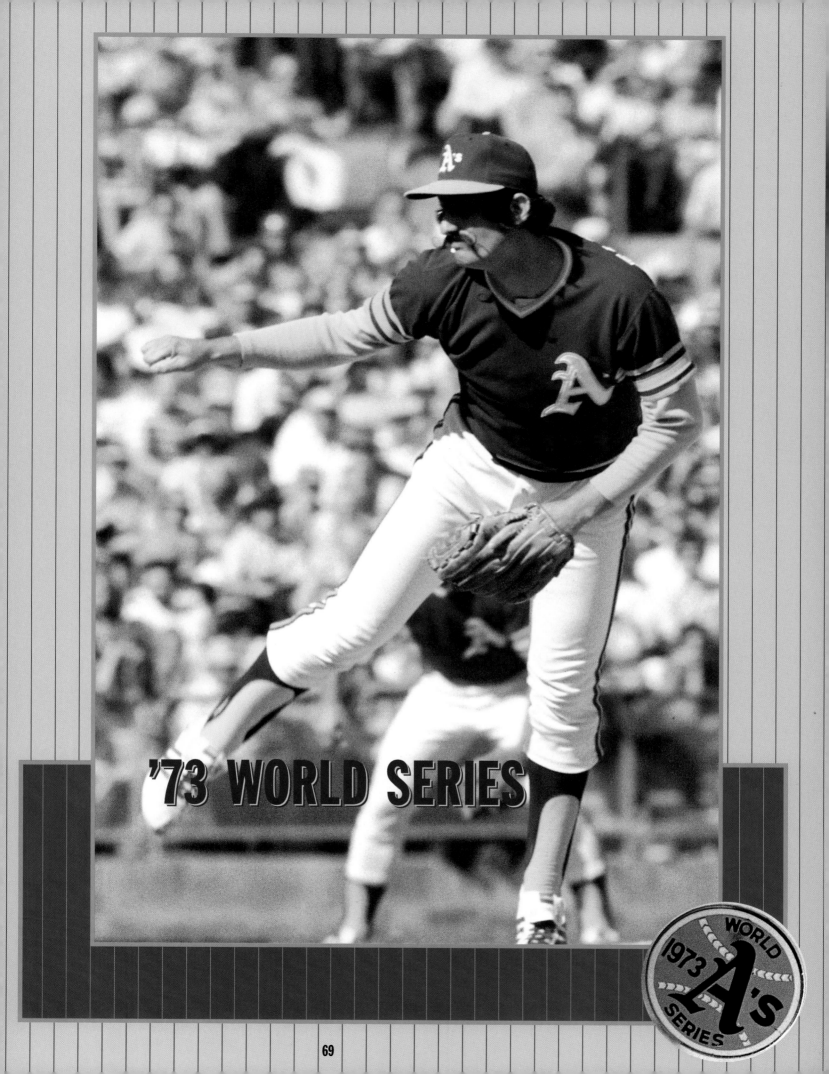

'73 WORLD SERIES

SAY HEY!
Mets
THE NEWS
NEW YORK'S PICTURE NEWSPAPER

Willie Mays spent his youth in New York, playing baseball with the Giants in the Polo Grounds, and, in his spare time, playing stickball with kids in the streets of Harlem. His return to the city in the spring of 1972 was nothing less than magical. "When you come back to New York," he said after the Mets acquired him from the Giants for a pitcher named Charlie Williams, "it's like coming back to paradise." In the first game he played in a Met uniform, Mays, 41, hit a home run to defeat his old team. "On a scale of 1 to 10 for drama," Bud Harrelson said, "I'd have to rate that about a 12."

On September 20, 1973, in the heat of the pennant race, Willie Mays announced his retirement, effective at the end of the season. "I thought I would be crying right now," he said at a press conference at Shea, "but I see so many of my friends, I can't cry. Maybe I'll cry tomorrow." Before he was done, he eked out two more game-winning hits—in the playoffs and World Series. At right, fans cheer Mays as he heads for the plate as a pinch-hitter in Game 5 of the '73 playoffs. As usual, he would deliver. "Baseball and me," he said, "we had what you would call a love affair."

No one has ever been less pretentious than Yogi Berra. After one memorable post-game interview, Milton Gross of the *New York Post* described the manager as "a semi-naked gnome." Berra would frequently invite reporters into his office while he was wearing nothing more than a pair of wire-framed glasses. It was not a pretty sight. "What the hell," Berra said, sucking on a brew. "Nobody's looking at me."

TOM TERRIFIC TO DR. K

1974-1984

75

Sullen and moody, or quiet and introspective? Nobody ever knew quite what to make of Dave Kingman, and that was fine with him. "I am a recluse," Kingman said. "By nature, I'm private. I never liked the front row. Notoriety doesn't come easily to me." Upon his return to the Mets in 1981, he presented every writer who followed the team with an engraved fountain pen as a peace offering. But his lack of regard for the media often bubbled to the surface. "I don't think I made myself controversial," he said. "I think the press made me controversial." His teammates didn't exactly love him. "Dave," said one, "has the personality of a tree trunk." The sign on his locker at Shea spoke volumes: "I'd rather be fishing."

Tom Seaver was gone, and Dwight Gooden was years away. When the Mets didn't have anything else to promote, they turned to Lee Mazzilli. It wasn't a bad choice; Mazzilli was good-looking, Italian American, a local boy, and he could hit. He even came up with his own marketing slogan, which the Mets turned into a poster that was pasted all over the five boroughs. "I'm Lee Mazzilli," the posters said, "and I want you to see what a kid from Brooklyn can do in Queens."

In what was not one of his brightest moves, in May of 1981 Frank Cashen traded reliever Jeff Reardon and Dan Norman to the Montreal Expos for disgruntled outfielder Ellis Valentine, whose best days were way behind him. Temperamental and thin-skinned, Valentine batted .288 with eight homers in 1982, he assured his departure when he called the Mets the worst organization in baseball. "How can a guy named Valentine be a jerk?" he asked reporters in spring training. Good question.

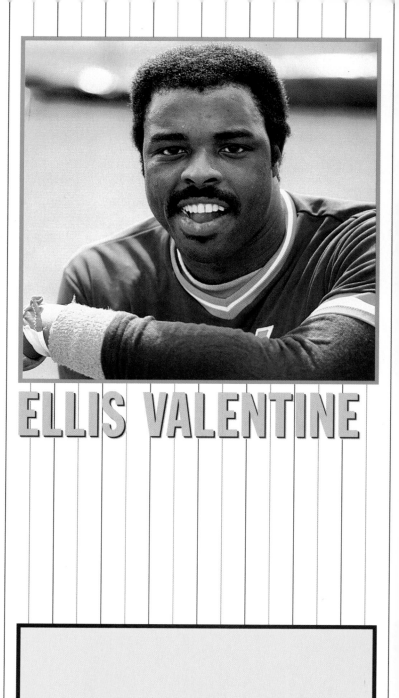

ELLIS VALENTINE

RANDY JONES

By the time Randy Jones arrived at Shea Stadium in 1981, he was a shadow of his former self. Once a master of control, he won the Cy Young Award with the lowly San Diego Padres in 1976, when he went 22-14 with a 2.74 ERA. That was before arm problems curtailed his effectiveness. Manager George Bamberger compared him to Mike Cuellar and Scott McGregor; instead, he pitched like nobody special, going 8-18 in two seasons before his release.

JOHN STEARNS

Long before Lenny Dykstra appropriated the term, John Stearns was the dude. As the Mets' catcher during the late '70s and early '80s, Stearns could strut with the best of them. His headfirst style excited the few who came out to see a last-place team. Better days were coming, but, sadly, Stearns would be gone. A devastating elbow injury in July 1982 destroyed his career. "I would have still been there, still been their catcher," he said in 1986. "Hubie Brooks would have been at third, and Gary Carter would have been in Montreal. I don't know why, but my body just blew out in my prime."

JOEL YOUNGBLOOD

He was a jack-of-all-trades who never got the chance to be th[e master of one]. Joel Youngblood could play just about anywhere, and usually did-the out[field one day, second base,] shortstop or third the next. "Youngblood's versatility," Joe To[rre said,] "is a manager's dream." Youngblood, who batted .350 and was the lone M[et all-star that] strike-bedeviled year, didn't agree. "It's a curse," he said. "What [wouldn't I give for] a regular job? Fall down on my knees and be[g?]

80

CRAIG SWAN

Injuries kept righthander Craig Swan from reaching his enormous potential. He suffered from appendicitis, peritonitis, a stress fracture of his pitching elbow, an ulcerated stomach, a torn rotator cuff, a broken rib suffered when he was hit in the back by a catcher's throw and a vicious boil under his right armpit. "Hey, you look like Burt Reynolds!" a female admirer once told him. "Burt Reynolds doesn't have a sore shoulder," Swan muttered under his breath.

GEORGE FOSTER

When laid-back George Foster signed a five-year, $10 million contract with the Mets in 1982, he lent a measure of respectability to a downtrodden team. "He was maybe the only legitimate major leaguer we had," general manager Frank Cashen later said. But by the time Foster and his legendary black bat were sent packing in the dog days of August '86, his career and his reputation were in ruins. Frustrated with his declining role on the team, Foster opened up to Jim Corbett of the Gannett Westchester newspapers. "I'm not saying it's a racial thing," Foster said. "But that seems to be the case in sports these days. When a ball club can, they replace a George Foster or a Mookie Wilson with a more popular white player." Foster said his remarks were misinterpreted, as his replacement in left field, Kevin Mitchell, was black. But manager Davey Johnson told Cashen, "It's him or me," and Foster was released.

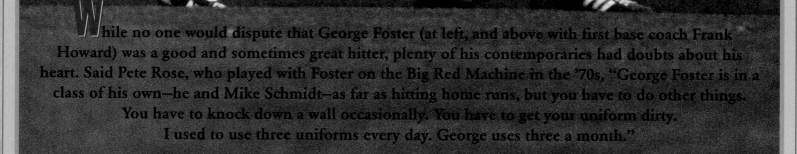

While no one would dispute that George Foster (at left, and above with first base coach Frank Howard) was a good and sometimes great hitter, plenty of his contemporaries had doubts about his heart. Said Pete Rose, who played with Foster on the Big Red Machine in the '70s, "George Foster is in a class of his own—he and Mike Schmidt—as far as hitting home runs, but you have to do other things. You have to knock down a wall occasionally. You have to get your uniform dirty. I used to use three uniforms every day. George uses three a month."

A drumroll, please. It's time for a brief discussion of the New York Mets' chronic problems at third base. Through the middle of the '94 season, 99 men had played the position, and few of them well. From Don Zimmer in 1962 to Bobby Bonilla in 1994, the hot corner has been a hot potato, tossed to an average of three new men a year. Hubie Brooks was the 69th third baseman in Mets history, and he may have been the best. Brooks was a decent fielder and a good clutch hitter, and he quickly became a fan favorite.

HUBIE BROOKS

His 24-game hitting streak in 1984 remains a club record; in appreciation, the Mets traded him to the Expos after the season in a package for Gary Carter. The team would miss his even-tempered presence in the clubhouse. In 1991, with the Mets drowning in a sea of bad attitudes, he was brought back for a last fling, but a high salary and a bad back combined to buy him another ticket out of town. He might be best remembered for his comment upon hearing that he had been dealt to Montreal: "Damn. Now I've got to face Dwight."

He could have earned the respect of his teammates merely by swinging the bat. "Straw is one of the few players in baseball," said Bob Ojeda, "who can carry a team. When he gets going good, it's contagious." But leading by example was not Darryl Strawberry's style. Instead, he demanded that the veterans pay attention to him. "If I'm the Mets' future or The Franchise," he said after his rookie season, "then I also want to be their leader. If nobody wants the job, I'll have to take it." The next spring, whenever he was late for a workout, the other players would snicker, "Here comes our leader."

He arrived at just the right time, a breath of fresh air for a team that had been choking on its own fumes. Mookie Wilson played all-out baseball, and he'd do anything to win. "You'd be surprised," he said, "how many ways there are to steal a run." He patrolled the outfield and raced around the bases for most of the decade, and he's still the Mets' all-time leader in steals (281) and triples (62).

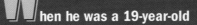

When he was a 19-year-old super-prospect in the Dodger organization, Bobby Valentine (above) once won a contest by eating 117 pancakes. He always loved to be the center of attention. By the time Valentine came to the Mets in 1977, his promising career had been ruined by injuries. But he could still talk a good game. Here he chats in the dugout with a couple of legendary New York sportswriters, Dick Young (left) and Milton Richman. 'I've tried to diversify the last few years," he said in '78, "but my thoughts and conversations always lead back to baseball." George Kalinsky remembers being impressed by the chatty Valentine, as well as by his opinionated company. "In this picture, Valentine is kidding around with two of the greatest writers that have ever covered the game," Kalinsky says. "To me, Dick Young was even more fascinating than the players he wrote about. He may have been the most influential baseball writer of his time."At right, pitcher Ed Lynch and broadcaster Tim McCarver share a private joke over an April 1984 *Sports Illustrated* cover story on Darryl Strawberry, "The Straw That Stirs The Mets." McCarver, a former catcher, joined Ralph Kiner in the booth for the 1983 season, and immediately livened things up. He would become a fixture at Shea Stadium and a regular in the clubhouse, known for his insight and his honesty. Lynch is now an assistant to Executive VP Joe McIlvaine.

DANNY HEEP

Danny Heep came to the Mets in December 1982, swapped by the Astros for a then obscure 27-year-old pitcher named Mike Scott. "Danny Heep is the most valuable player on our team," Davey Johnson said of the outfielder/first baseman after the 1984 season. "He can fill in on a number of positions. He certainly gives us flexibility." Heep's best season was 1985, when he hit .280 and became Nolan Ryan's 4,000th strikeout victim. "It's not easy for me," he said. "It never has been."

DWIGHT GOODEN

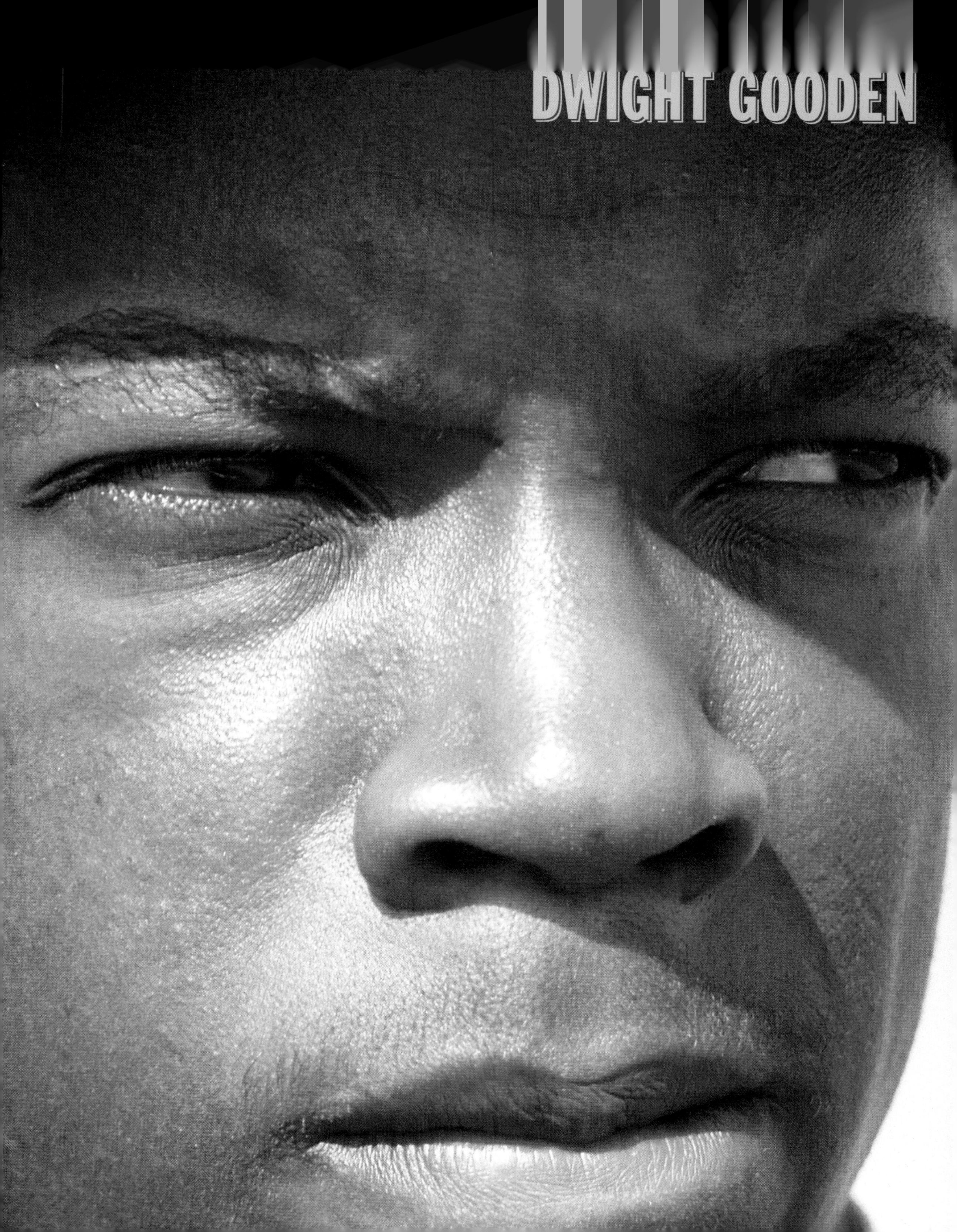

As an 18-year-old in Class A ball, Dwight Gooden struck out 300 batters in 191 innings. Now, in the spring of 1984, the 19-year-old phenom was about to face major leaguers for the first time. It was an intrasquad game at old Huggins-Stengel Field in St. Petersburg, Florida, and the backstop was surrounded by reporters and scouts. Gooden went out to the mound and threw his first warmup pitch. It buzzed through the air like a swarm of bees. One scout closed his notebook. "I've seen enough," he said.

94

Tom Seaver with Dwight Gooden

For an all-too-brief period, Dwight Gooden owned New York. His motion was captured on a 10-story mural that greeted visitors to the West Side of midtown Manhattan. His nickname, Dr. K, was registered as a trademark. His curveball was dubbed Lord Charles. He even became a rapper for a day, adding flair to a song called Get Mets-merized: "Dwight's my name/What can I say?/You know they call me Doctor K/Changeup, fastball/Slider and curve/Step up to the plate/If ya' got the nerve."

ANOTHER MIRACLE

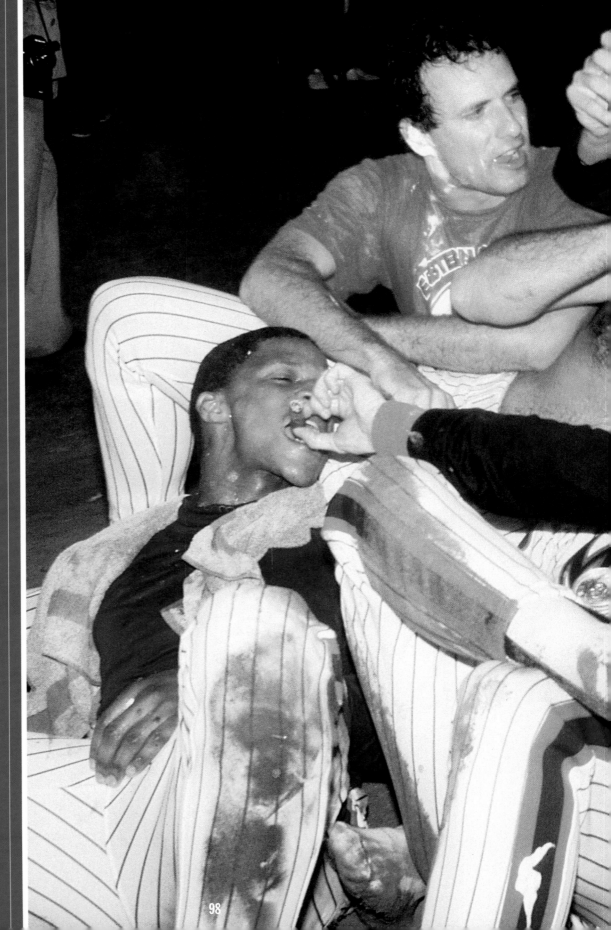

As a high school senior, Darryl Strawberry was compared to Ted Williams. "He's the best prospect I've seen in the last 30 years," said Hugh Alexander, a scout for the Philadelphia Phillies. "A hellacious talent," said Frank Cashen, who made sure the Mets selected Strawberry with the No. 1 pick in the 1980 draft. He breezed through the minors and hit New York ahead of schedule, winning the National League Rookie of the Year award in 1983. By 1985, he was an integral part of a team that was rapidly becoming something special. Here, with Keith Hernandez (foreground) and Gary Carter (right), the Straw celebrates an early-season homer.

Six times, the Mets and St. Louis Cardinals faced off during the heat of the 1985 pennant race. Six times, the games came down to the last at-bat. On September 12, the rubber match of a three-game set at Shea, the Mets had blown a 6-0 lead. Tied 6-6 in the bottom of the ninth, Mookie Wilson led off. "We needed a quick lift," he said. "I needed to get on, somehow." Wilson hit a chopper behind the mound, where shortstop Ozzie Smith grabbed it, but his throw to first was low. Wally Backman bunted Wilson over, and then Keith Hernandez singled to left. Wilson scored standing up, giving the Mets a one-game lead in the Eastern Division. "This," Hernandez said, "was a real test of our character." The Cardinals would win the race, but in '86 the Mets won the war.

Less than a year after helping the St. Louis Cardinals win the 1982 World Series, Keith Hernandez went from the penthouse to the outhouse: He was traded to the Mets. "At the time," he later said, "I thought I was going to Siberia." Indeed, the Mets finished last in '83, but won 90 games the following season, and the championship in '86. "I was traded to a club that was a perennial loser," said the man his teammates called Mex, a nickname he loved, particularly since his ancestors were Scottish and Spanish. "To see it turn around, to be a part of that, is a very prideful feeling."

KEITH HERNANDEZ

Like many players, Keith Hernandez wouldn't touch his face with a razor blade until after a night game, if at all. Along with his mustache, the stubble became his trademark. "I just don't like to shave," he said. "Can't shave every day, it beats my face up. I normally let it grow for three or four days, and sometimes I forget and it stays there longer. I never shave in the morning, because if I shave in the morning and play at night, I go out there and sweat and my face breaks out in a rash."

Hernandez was a creature of habit. Nearly four hours before a night game, he'd be in the clubhouse, half-dressed, playing cards or doing *The New York Times*' crossword puzzle, in ink. At around 4:30, sipping coffee and puffing on a Winston, he'd begin holding court with the writers and broadcasters who would gather around his stall. By the time batting practice began, he would have worked his way through a pack of cigarettes. After the game, as many as two dozen reporters would wait to interview him, pens scratching and tape recorders whirring. "Hold on, let me get a cigarette," he'd say to the assembled. 'O.K., let me get a beer. O.K., now I'm ready."

As a hitter, Hernandez had the uncanny ability to deliver in the clutch. As a fielder, he was nonpareil, the winner of 11 Gold Gloves, so acrobatic that Tim McCarver dubbed him "the Baryshnikov of first basemen." By 1987, Davey Johnson acknowledged the obvious and appointed him the Mets' first captain. The letter C was sewn onto the front of his jersey. "I perceive my job as a leader as setting the example on the field," Hernandez once said. "I'm not going to yell at anybody. The best example I can set is to play hard every day with aches and pains and play to win. That's a good enough example right there."

Gary Carter had a flair for the dramatic. In his first game as a Met in 1985, he hit a 10th-inning homer to beat the Cardinals at Shea. In Game 6 of the '86 Series, his two-out single ignited the Mets' last-ditch comeback. But in the end, his career in New York just kind of petered out. Injuries led to a .183 batting average in just 50 games in '89; two days after the end of that season, Carter and co-captain Hernandez both were released. "I came here on a mission to nurture a young pitching staff, and to win a World Series," he said. Mission accomplished.

GARY CARTER

Baseball scouts call it "the good face." Gary Carter was the poster child. "A born-again smile freak," said the Spaceman, Bill Lee, a teammate in Montreal. You had to get close to that smiling face to observe one of its most interesting qualities: The iris of Carter's right eye is half-brown and half-green, the colors divided on a diagonal. It's a condition so rare that it doesn't have a name. "I'm just unique," Carter said with—you guessed it!—a grin.

Before every game, Carter would stand on a table in the trainer's room and get wrapped like a mummy. To make the situation slightly more comfortable, a ceiling tile was removed to make room for his head. "By the time they finish with him," Frank Cashen said, "Gary looks like a gladiator." Maybe so, but he felt more like an aging catcher who'd had surgery on both knees and countless cortisone injections to ease the pain and swelling. "I've never had so many foul tips and nicks," he said late in the summer of '87. "I've never had so many parts of my body hurt from time to time. And it's getting more difficult, because my body doesn't heal as quickly." He caught 135 games that year.

Rafael Santana (left), Wally Backman and Howard Johnson.

KEVIN MITCHELL

The Mets didn't know what to do with Kevin Mitchell. So, in 1986, they asked the 24-year-old rookie to do it all. Mitchell played nearly everywhere—all three outfield positions, shortstop, first and third—and made a significant contribution to the team's championship season, batting .277 with 12 home runs. "Believe it or not," he said, "I like this. I like coming to the park every day, wondering, 'Where am I going to play today?' I like my role. It's different."

JOE McILVAINE

FRANK CASHEN

RON DARLING

P art Chinese, part Hawaiian and part French, with a strong right arm, a Yale education and a winning attitude, Ron Darling was all over New York in the mid-'80s. He went out with Madonna. He appeared on the cover of *GQ*. One women's magazine named him one of the 10 sexiest men in America. His teammates named him Mr. Perfect. He received dozens of letters a day, many of which contained brazen propositions. He dated and later married Irish-born model Toni O'Reilly, but that didn't faze his admirers.

W hether he was running to the mound to congratulate Dwight Gooden on a game-ending strikeout—"You're the best, Doc! You're the best!"—or simply hanging around the clubhouse playing cards, Gary Carter was the pitcher's best friend. "You've got to pump up the pitchers, and keep 'em pumped, even when the game's over," Carter said. "It's one of the good catcher's most important responsibilities." For the most part, the pitchers appreciated the attention. "Before Gary came here," said Ron Darling, "we were a pretty good team. But he made us great."

ROGER McDOWELL

Although Roger McDowell had a well-deserved reputation as a clown, there was a method to his madness. "It keeps me loose," said the gum-popping, slider-tossing righthander. "A relief pitcher lives with ups and downs. You're always under pressure, sometimes day after day. You have to have a different type of personality." Like Tug McGraw before him, he wore it well.

After the 1986 World Series, Mookie Wilson visited the New York Stock Exchange with members of Mookie's Roses, the New Jersey club for disadvantaged teenage girls that he founded with his wife, Rosa. When he was spotted in the balcony, the traders stopped their frantic activity and began chanting his name: Mookie! Mookie! "They didn't even do that for Ronald Reagan," one observer said. When he was traded to the Toronto Blue Jays in 1989, Wilson reflected on '86. "That season was my best memory of New York," he said. "It was the peak."

If Keith Hernandez was the heart and soul of the '86 Mets, then Wally Backman was the gristle. Whether he was turning a double play or breaking one up, Backman played with little regard for his own safety. "If I'm in the trenches, I want Wally in my foxhole," Hernandez said. "He's one of the greatest competitors I've ever seen." Backman, who batted a career-high .320 that championship season, described himself as hard-nosed. "If I had to cut off a finger to win a ball game, I'd do it." Fortunately, it never came to that.

D arryl Stra... looked like a professional, but... he didn't act like one. Not long after... advanced from Triple-A to the... the whispers began. He ... a hard... the... said. He didn't care about making the most of his talent. ... one day... coach Bill Robinson once said, "when Darryl just doesn't feel like taking fly balls in outfield practice, I've told him, 'With the money you're getting, it behooves you to bust your butt on every play.' The sun doesn't rise and set on ...." Responded Straw, "I know in my heart that every time I step on the field, I play hard and I play to win."

Howard Johnson and Darryl Strawberry celebrate at home plate.

THE WINNING RUN

1962 Mets 25th 1986 ANNIVERSARY ®

Bill Buckner watched the Mets' celebration in utter disbelief. "I can't remember the last time I missed a ground ball," said the dignified veteran. "I'll remember that one for a long time."

METS 6, RED SOX 5

The champagne was quietly wheeled out of the visitors' clubhouse.

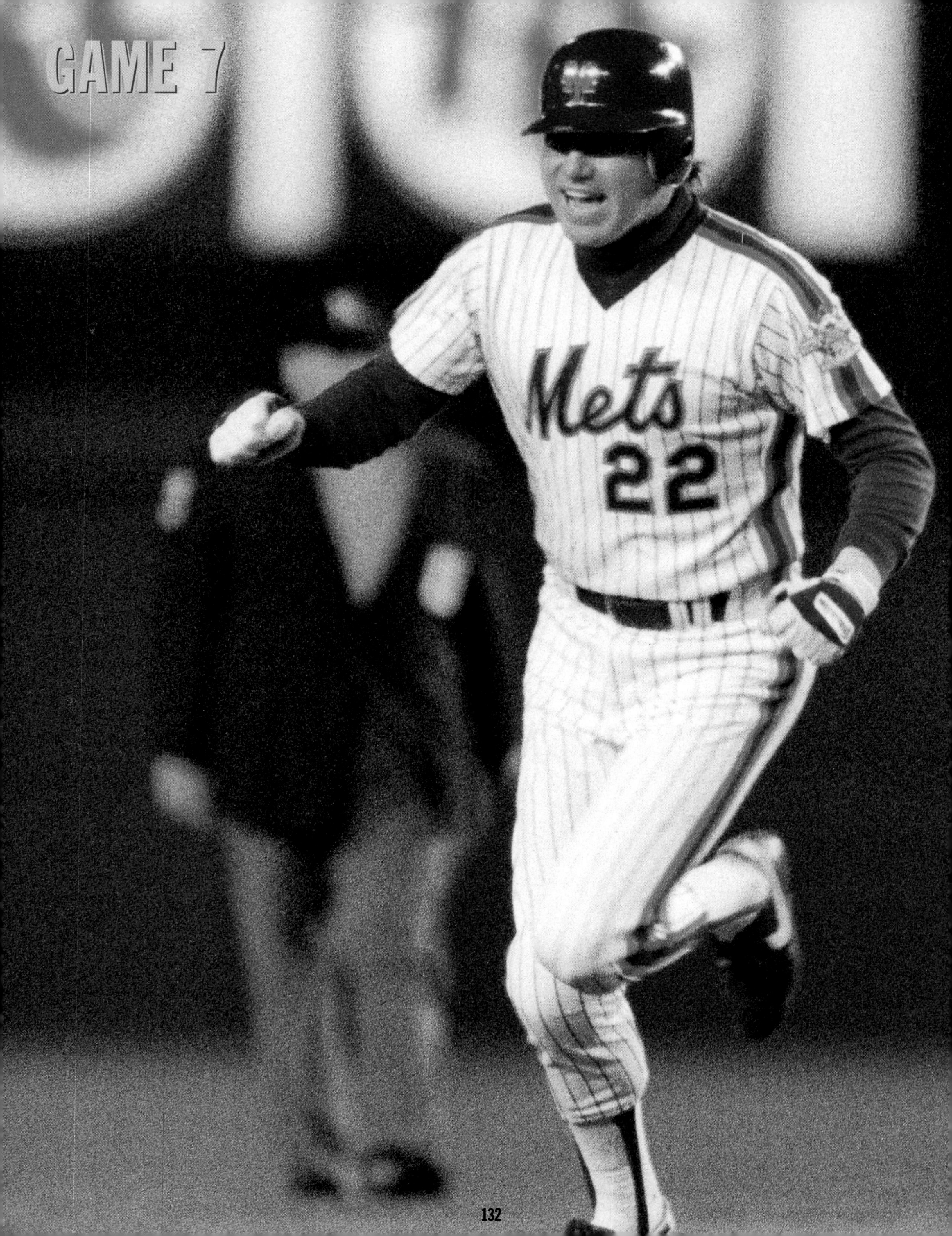
Mets
22

In the seventh inning of the seventh game of the 1986 World Series, Ray Knight, whose two-out, two-strike single had saved the Mets in Game 6, broke a 3-3 tie with a leadoff homer. It would prove to be a decisive blow. Knight leaped with joy. "Rounding the bases after that homer was a special feeling," he said. "But maybe what felt even better was scoring the winner in Game 6. I was rounding third base and Buddy Harrelson was there, yelling, 'Go, go, go!' It was just a total, unbelievable feeling."

When Knight got to the dugout after his seventh-inning homer, he made a point to spot his wife, golfer Nancy Lopez, in the stands. Then he blew her a kiss. After the game, Lopez said she wasn't surprised by her husband's big Knight. "He got a lot of rest and slept late before he left for Shea. I told him if he played as good as he looked, he'd get three hits and a home run. I was close, wasn't I?"

WORLD CHAMPIONS

Two ambitions, among many, converged at 11:26 P.M. on October 27, 1986, when Jesse Orosco flung his glove in the air to celebrate the end of the 1986 World Series. Orosco came to the Mets in 1979 as the player to be named later in a trade for Jerry Koosman, who ironically had recorded the last out of the '69 Series. "If you ever get the chance to throw the last pitch," Orosco said, "that's a dream come true." So is the chance to take the last picture, the one that sums up a season, perhaps even a franchise, in one frame. George Kalinsky was shooting from the photographer's box on the third-base side. "Orosco had his back to me when he jumped in the air, and I thought to myself, 'That's it. the shot's blown.' But then he miraculously turned my way and fell to his knees," Kalinsky remembers. "It's all luck. If he's not facing me, there's no picture."

THE AGONY OF DEFEAT

For the vanquished Red Sox and their long-suffering fans, losing the World Series was an excruciating blow. They had it won, and they let it slip away. While the Mets whooped it up on the field, Wade Boggs cried quietly on the bench.

CHAMPAGNE FOR EVERYONE

In New York, when you're a winner, the bandwagon can get pretty crowded. Here, Mayor Ed Koch baptizes Ray Knight in the clubhouse of the 1986 World Champions.

It seemed like there were a million people celebrating in the clubhouse. And with the showers running, the sweat dripping and the champagne flowing, moisture was fogging up everything. But before George Kalinsky's camera lens was obscured, he captured Tim McCarver and Wally Backman roaring in delight as a huge bucket of ice was dumped on Keith Hernandez— apparently in an effort to cool him off.

Like Yogi Berra, they said, he didn't have control of the team. Like Casey Stengel, they said, he was only as good as his players. But like Gil Hodges, Davey Johnson (far left) managed the Mets to the World Series championship. Writing in *The Washington Post,* Thomas Boswell captured the tenor of the times: "Johnson manages the team with the sanest direction and the zaniest players in baseball...a bottomless talent pool of reformed substance abusers, prima donnas, glory hounds, media darlings, braggarts, barroom brawlers, fatsos and crybabies." Somehow, in his laid-back way, Johnson became the winningest manager in franchise history. "It's not easy," he reflected after he was fired in 1990, "to run a ball club in New York."

World Champions Bob Ojeda, Howard Johnson and Ron Darling enjoy a champagne shampoo.

After coming close in 1984 and closer in '85, Davey Johnson threw down the gauntlet in the spring of '86. "I expect us to win," he said. "But I don't want just to win the division. I want to dominate it. They can call it arrogance if they want. I call it confidence." Six months later, Johnson (right) was riding in a victory parade down lower Broadway, seated in an open car between Mayor Ed Koch and Governor Mario Cuomo. "All I'm thinking about now," he said after winning Game 7 and the World Series, "is savoring this moment for a long time." Ray Knight (below at left, with Joe McIlvaine) didn't know it yet, but these fleeting moments in the champagne-drenched clubhouse would be his last as a Met. He wanted a two-year deal. The Mets offered him one year. And the next thing you knew, the MVP was gone. He signed with the Orioles as a free agent, and the Mets mailed him his championship ring.

ON THE STEPS OF CITY HALL

In the fall of '86, Mookie Wilson was in constant demand as a speaker. A few weeks after the victory celebration and the ticker-tape parade through the canyons of lower Manhattan, he traveled to the University of Massachusetts, where a brawl between white Red Sox fans and black Mets fans had occurred after Game 7. "You can't change the way society has treated people before now," he told an multiracial audience of more than 1,000 students. "But you can be force on what happens from now on. I've learned through the years not to be worried about race. If you look for what's wrong in people, you'll find it. My motto is to look for what's right in people. That's easier."

Foreground, right: Co-owner Fred Wilpon and his wife, Judy, beam as Wilson revs up the crowd at the Mets' victory celebration on the steps of City Hall.

IN SEARCH OF ANOTHER MIRACLE

On the scoreboard:

17	1B	
8	C	
18	RF	
22	LF	
20	3B	
3	SS	
19	P	

ATL		42
STL		30
CHI		40
LA		34
HOU		39
SD		32
SF		29

HP 24 101h

1987-1994

On opening day of the '87 season, Frank Cashen (with bow tie), co-owner Nelson Doubleday (with sunglasses) and NL President Bart Giamatti (at right) present manager Davey Johnson with his World Series ring.

GREGG JEFFERIES

Switch-hitting Gregg Jefferies was going to be The Franchise. Subjecting the two-time Baseball America Minor League Player of the Year to unbearable pressure, the Mets groomed him as a shortstop and third baseman, then asked him to play second base. Manager Davey Johnson took a special interest, which earned Jefferies the enmity of his teammates. "The guys acted like I had a disease," said Jefferies, who was traded to the Royals after the 1991 season. "I felt like an outsider. I know a lot of guys that are glad I'm gone. I don't care. I won't miss what I went through."

After falling to second place in 1987, the Mets won their fourth Eastern Division title with a 100-60 record in '88. Ron Darling pitched a complete game in the clincher September 22 as the Mets beat the Phillies 3-1 at Shea. An aging Gary Carter hit just .242 with 11 homers (including the 300th of his career) and 46 RBIs.

NL EAST CHAMPS 1988

The 1988 NL Championship Series will be remembered as the beginning of the Mets' five-year slide toward oblivion. In the ninth inning of Game 4 at Shea, with the home team on the verge of taking a virtually insurmountable 3-1 lead over the Los Angeles Dodgers, Dwight Gooden gave up a two-run, game-tying homer to Mike Scioscia. The Dodgers won it on Kirk Gibson's home run in the 12th to knot the series. In Game 5, Gibson's three-run homer in the fifth (left), triggered a celebration (above) and keyed a 7-4 Dodger win. The Mets eventually lost the series in seven, and haven't played a post-season game since.

When he was hit in the lower back by this pitch on July 8, 1989, scrappy infielder Tim Teufel decided he had had enough of Reds reliever Rob Dibble. Teufel, whose last name means devil in German, charged the mound and took a couple of swings at the cocky Dibble, touching off a benches-clearing brawl.

DAVE MAGADAN

First basemen and third basemen are supposed to be able to take 'em deep. That's something Dave Magadan was rarely able to do. So, despite a .292 career average, the polite, photogenic Magadan was never able to get the at-bats to establish himself as a star. At the end of the 1992 season, the Mets let him go to the Florida Marlins. Asked how he felt about joining an expansion team, Magadan laughed. "I felt like I played for an expansion team last season," he said.

DAVID CONE

He may have looked like a choirboy, but David Cone liked to raise a little hell. He was outspoken. He was a loose cannon. He found himself in embarrassing situations now and then. But he was also a winner. "This is the end of an era," Cone said when he was traded to Toronto in 1992. "I'm the last link to the mid-'80s Arrogant Mets. This trade shows that they're going in a different direction. Obviously, the club has taken a step backwards. It's going to be a long, hard road."

For three years at St. John's they were teammates and friends. Then, in 1990, John Franco and Frank Viola were reunited as Mets. "We're the Big East section of the clubhouse," chirped Franco, who combined with Viola to lead the Redmen to the College World Series in 1981. "In those days," said Viola, a native of Hempstead, L.I., "people didn't know that St. John's could play baseball." Now they know.

Everybody was talking about Howard Johnson in 1987, when he hit 36 homers, triple his career high. St. Louis Cardinals manager Whitey Herzog, among others, claimed that Johnson was corking his bats, igniting a furor that didn't abate until one of the bats was confiscated and irradiated. The X-rays, as Dizzy Dean might have put it, showed nothing. Still, Johnson, who also stole 32 bases that year, was forced on the defensive, which took the fun out of his first big year. "Everybody picked at me," he said, "like they thought I couldn't be doing it unless I was doing something wrong."

HOWARD JOHNSON

The critics said he couldn't play third base. In the end, they were right. But oh, how Howard Johnson tried. "I'm not the best defensive player in the world," said Johnson, who also played shortstop, right field and center field on a regular basis at one time or another. "I'm not the worst, either." Said Bud Harrelson, "HoJo's got the best arm, the best speed and the best power of any third baseman the Mets have ever had."

In November 1990, the Mets let the franchise player walk. He turned down their offer of $15 million for four years, accepting a $20 million, five-year contract from the Los Angeles Dodgers. His legacy, at best, is mixed. "The man had such marvelous potential, and it was never realized," said Frank Cashen. "He's been a good player, not a great player. So he's gone. And I think we'll be able to plant some new seeds in the old Strawberry field."

BUD HARRELSON

Bud Harrelson, one of the most popular players to wear a Mets uniform, replaced Davey Johnson as manager in May 1990 with the team floundering in fourth place. The Mets responded to the change and battled the Pirates down to the wire before Pittsburgh captured the Eastern title by four games. The Mets fell out of contention the following year, and Harrelson was let go with a week remaining in the season. "I came in with a smile," he said before he got the axe, "and I'll go out with a smile." Harrelson now serves the Mets as a Community Outreach Representative.

WILLIE RANDOLPH

In the twilight of a great career, Willie Randolph, the man who electrified
rallies for the Yankees in the '70s and '80s, came back to New York to play second base for the Mets. "I'd be
kidding you if I said I didn't feel the aches and pains," Randolph 38, said in 1992.
"When I was younger, after a game I'd get dressed and go. Now you take your Advil and get in the whirlpool,
but when I'm right, I can still play." He batted .252 that season, then joined the Yankees
as an executive vice president and later became their third base coach.

BRET SABERHAGEN

When the Mets scouted Bret Saberhagen in 1991, the Kansas City righthander was wielding a 97-mph fastball. "When you see that," said Mets GM Al Harazin, who traded Kevin McReynolds, Gregg Jefferies and Keith Miller to the Royals for Saberhagen and Bill Pecota in December 1991, "you get goosebumps." But in '92 and '93, all Saberhagen gave the Mets was grief, going 10-12. In '93, he threw firecrackers at several reporters, and squirted bleach on several others.

'Why grow up?" he said in '94. "This is supposed to be fun." Saberhagen rebounded to make the All-Star team in his third season as a Met.

BOBBY BONILLA

He liked to portray himself as a son of New York who loved the city and was glad to be home. But for Bobby Bonilla, the spotlight was often unflattering. His relationship with fans and the media was stormy at best. "I have my smile," he told reporters after he signed a five-year, $29 million contract with the Mets in December 1991, "and it's going to be hard to knock it off. I know you'll try."

How could it happen? How could a 27-year-old pitcher with a live right arm lose a major league record 27 games in a row during the '92 and '93 seasons? Asked repeatedly to explain, Anthony Young was, well, at a loss. "It was a disaster, a nightmare for me and the Mets," said Young, who was dignified in defeat and exuberant when, on July 28, 1993, he pitched one shaky inning of relief and finally earned a victory. "But it's over with. I don't even want to look back."

172

He won the Cy Young Award in 1985, but Dwight Gooden seems proudest of his silver bats, which are given to the player with the highest batting average at each position. When the manager is looking down the bench for a pinch-hitter, Gooden has been known to don a batting helmet, just in case. "If I could play every day, I think I could hit .290," he said. "Mostly singles and doubles, and maybe seven home runs, 10 tops. I'd take a home run over a no-hitter any day. Man, I've got to get more ABs." He's still waiting.

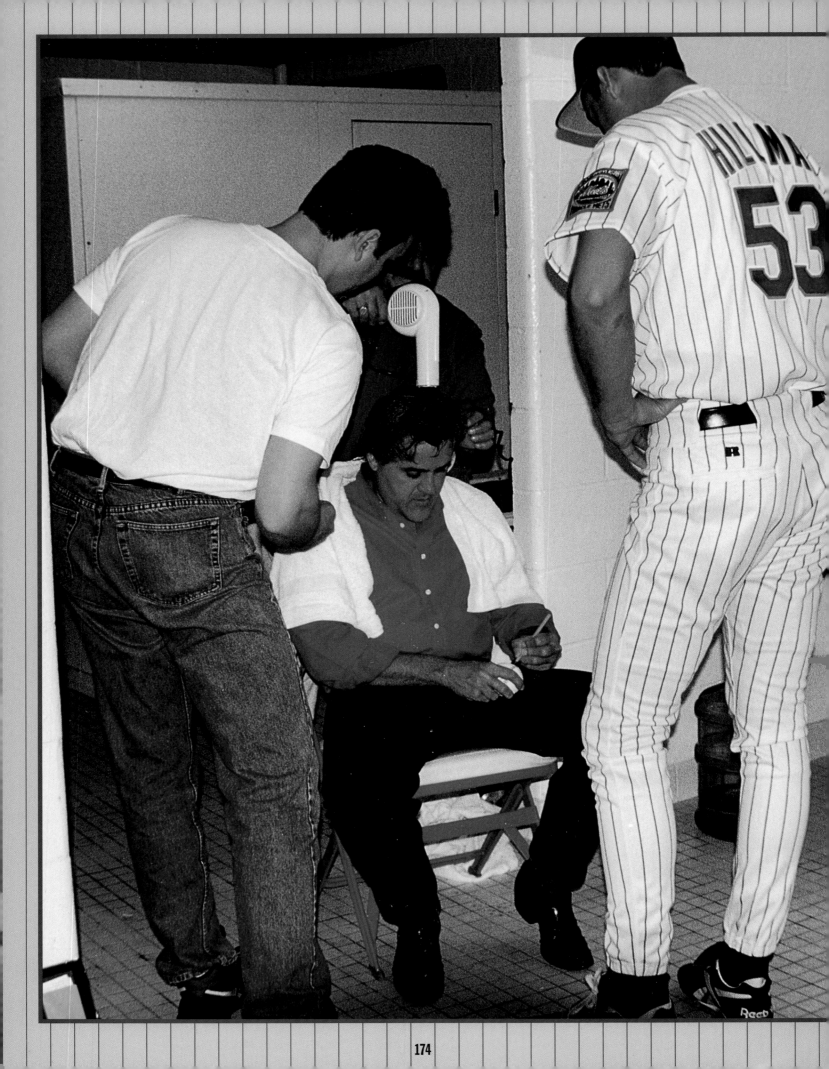

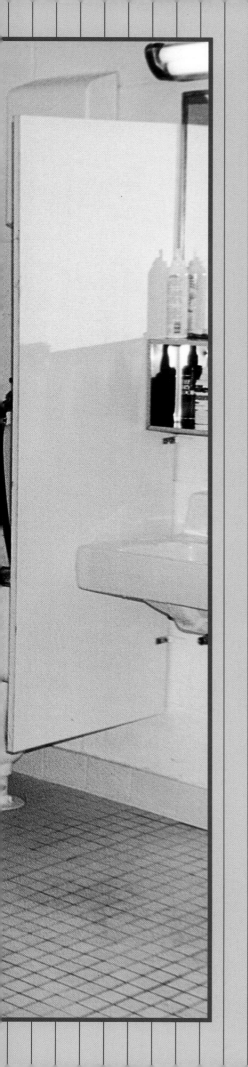

During their abysmal 1993 season, the Mets were a national joke, the butt of cruel but often funny late-night monologues by David Letterman and Jay Leno (left). While Letterman kept his distance, Leno bravely ventured into the Mets' clubhouse in May 1994, giving the players a chance to get even. Invited to take part in a so-called three-man lift, in which reliever John Franco supposedly would hoist three people off the floor at once, Leno took up his position, only to be doused with soda, shaving cream, water and shampoo. "I had a feeling some kind of scam was going on," said Leno, who good-naturedly dried off and signed autographs.

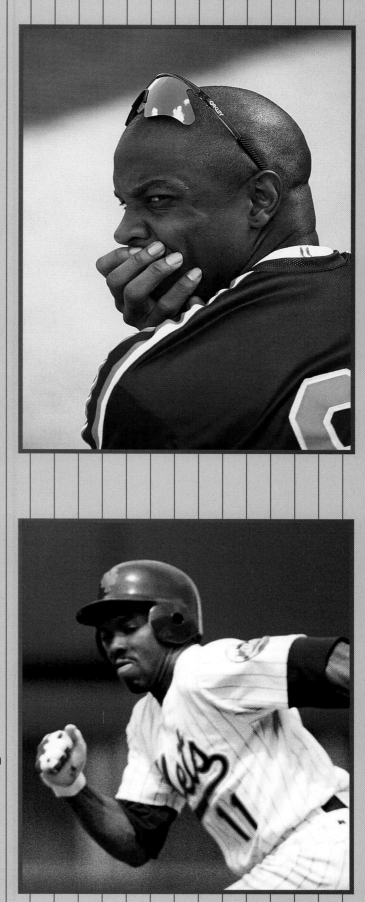

Forget about Ryan for Fregosi. The four-year, $12 million contract the Mets gave Vince Coleman in December 1990 will go down in history as the worst deal the club ever made. General Manager Frank Cashen thought he would replace Darryl Strawberry's power with Coleman's speed. Instead, he merely added another surly, malevolent presence to a clubhouse that was already crackling with ill will. Early in the '93 season, Coleman accidentally whacked Dwight Gooden (top) with a golf club, causing him to miss a start. After Coleman tossed a firecracker at fans outside Dodger Stadium in July 1993, injuring a two-year-old girl, he would never again play for the team.

JOSE VIZCAINO

The Mets needed a shortstop and a leadoff hitter. The Cubs were looking for a pitcher. So Anthony Young for Jose Vizcaino was the perfect trade. "Jose fit into our situation just like a glove," said manager Dallas Green. "He's already part of our foundation." For his part, Vizcaino was thrilled. His seven cousins, a brother and a sister had migrated to New York from the Dominican Republic. "I'm happy to be here," he said. "Now I have an opportunity to play."

RYAN THOMPSON

The camera loves Ryan Thompson. "I keep telling him," George Kalinsky says, "if he hits as well as he smiles, he's going to be a superstar." Now, every time he has a big game, Thompson offers the photographer a big grin. "See," he says, "my hitting's catching up!"

When the Mets traded David Cone to the Blue Jays for Jeff Kent and Ryan Thompson, they were criticized for making what looked like a bum deal. "That trade doesn't look so lopsided now," Cone said in 1994, when asked about Kent's hot bat. A feisty perfectionist, Kent is striving to improve his play at second base, a position he intends to hold for a long time. "I'm the perfect New Yorker," says Kent, the son of a Southern California police lieutenant. "I'm a hard-ass. I take no bull. I work hard, and I hate to lose. What more could you ask for?"

JEFF KENT

DAVID SEGUI

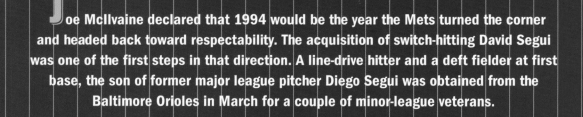

J oe McIlvaine declared that 1994 would be the year the Mets turned the corner and headed back toward respectability. The acquisition of switch-hitting David Segui was one of the first steps in that direction. A line-drive hitter and a deft fielder at first base, the son of former major league pitcher Diego Segui was obtained from the Baltimore Orioles in March for a couple of minor-league veterans.

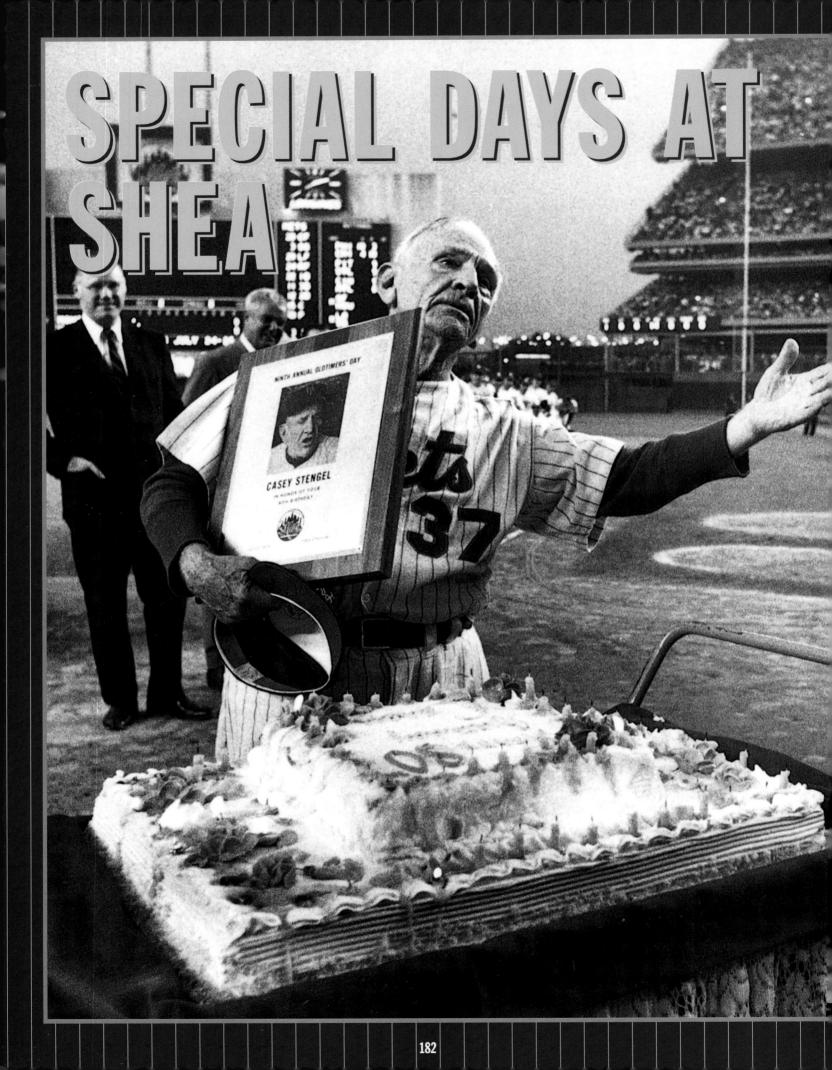

SPECIAL DAYS AT SHEA

NINTH ANNUAL OLDTIMERS' DAY

CASEY STENGEL

IN HONOR OF YOUR
80th BIRTHDAY

Casey Stengel and broadcaster Lindsey Nelson had a memorable relationship. Their mutual interviews were always entertaining, but perhaps the best occurred during the first week of the '62 season, when Nelson asked Casey to run down the starting lineup. Stengel's train of thought derailed in right field: "He's a splendid man and he knows how to do it. He's been around and he swings the bat there in right field and he knows what to do. He's got a big family and he wants to provide for them, and he's a fine outstanding player, the fella in right field. You can be sure he'll be ready when the bell rings, and that's his name—[Gus] Bell!"

By the time he started appearing at Shea for Old-Timers' Games, Jackie Robinson (far right) actually looked like an old-timer. It was hard to believe that his career with the Brooklyn Dodgers had ended less than a decade before. The lines on his face and the gray in his hair belied the stress he had to cope with during his playing days. In 1947, he broke the color barrier, becoming the first black man to play in the modern major leagues. But Robinson wasn't the only old Brooklyn Dodger to come to Shea for visits. Here, Don Newcombe, the powerful righthander who dazzled Brooklyn fans in the '50s, patiently signs autographs for admirers. Newcombe's career was undone by personal problems, but he would later strive to steer major leaguers away from the rocky path he had followed, becoming an effective crusader against alcoholism.

In 1947, it could be argued, Leo Durocher helped make Gil Hodges a major leaguer, when the Brooklyn Dodgers' manager strongly suggested that the gawky backup catcher ~~learn to play first base~~. In 1969, it could be argued, Gil Hodges helped unmake Leo Durocher as a major league manager, when the Miracle Mets overtook the favored Chicago Cubs and ruined Durocher's last, best chance to get back to the World Series. "There's no way," he sputtered late in the season, "the Mets can go on this way."
But he was wrong. Here, at a game between the Mets and the Cubs on Old-Timers' Day at Shea in 1971, Hodges and Durocher get together with an old Brooklyn teammate, Clyde King. Less than a year later, Hodges would suffer a fatal heart attack two days shy of his 48th birthday.

187

During the 28 seasons George Weiss was farm director and general manager, the New York Yankees won 19 American League pennants and 15 World Series. Itchy in retirement—"I married George for better or for worse," said his wife, Hazel, "but not for lunch"—Weiss (right, with Yogi Berra) returned in 1961 to spend six more years building a new New York team, the Mets. "He knew how to pick men," said Casey Stengel, his longtime associate. Weiss earned this reputation in 1935, when he convinced Yankees owner Jacob Ruppert to spend the princely sum of $25,000 to purchase the contract of a gimpy-legged minor league outfielder named Joe DiMaggio. Observed Weiss, "I never made a better deal."

188

When the Giants left for San Francisco, it killed me," said Joan Whitney Payson, who sank a small portion of her large fortune into a new National League franchise for New York. She became the Mets' first lady, impressing her constituency with charm and sincerity. She admitted that manager Casey Stengel (shown here greeting her) was perplexing at times. "If only I knew what he was talking about," she would say with a shake of her head.

ontrary to the impression he gave, Satchel Paige wasn't born an old-timer.
In his day, he may have been even better than Tom Seaver, whom he posed with during Old-
Timers' Day festivities one year. But Old Satch's best years were spent in the relative
obscurity of the Negro Leagues, an injustice that will forever weigh heavily
on the conscience of the game.

"Old-Timers' games are like airplane landings," Casey Stengel said. "If you can walk away from them, they're successful." The Mets would bring the old man out on the field in various contraptions— a horse and buggy one year, a stagecoach the next. In 1975, a few months before his death and suffering from painful cancer of the lymph nodes, Stengel was carted onto the field in a chariot, dressed, of course, in his familiar number 37. He had the strength to offer a wink and a wave. Soon, at 85, he was history.

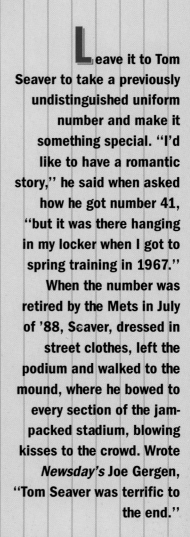

Leave it to Tom Seaver to take a previously undistinguished uniform number and make it something special. "I'd like to have a romantic story," he said when asked how he got number 41, "but it was there hanging in my locker when I got to spring training in 1967." When the number was retired by the Mets in July of '88, Seaver, dressed in street clothes, left the podium and walked to the mound, where he bowed to every section of the jam-packed stadium, blowing kisses to the crowd. Wrote *Newsday's* Joe Gergen, "Tom Seaver was terrific to the end."

ED KRANEPOOL

As a part-time stockbroker, Ed Kranepool, the last of the Original Mets, couched his expectations for the '69 season in Wall Street lingo. "There will be slumps," he told Joseph Durso, "and maybe even a sell-off by the Fourth of July. But generally, I'm optimistic." Maybe even psychic. Kranepool, pictured here at a recent Old-Timers' Day, noted that during the World Series every year the Dow Jones ticker provided regular updates on the games. "Wouldn't it be great," he mused, "if the Mets got into the Series and I hit a home run that was flashed over the ticker along with the quotations? Boy, the office would go wild." It happened in Game 3.

RON HUNT

Best known for his tendency to get hit by pitches, Ron Hunt was the first Met to start for the National League in the All-Star Game. He was selected for the honor in 1964, a season in which the second baseman batted .303. In his rookie year, 1963, Hunt was plunked 13 times—a club record. "He stands up there better than a lot of my veterans," said an admiring Casey Stengel. "He really digs in." Traded to the Dodgers in 1967, Hunt also played for the Giants, Expos and Cardinals. In a 12-year career, he was hit 243 times, a National League record.

Willie Mays used to be a frequent guest on Old-Timers' Day at Shea. When he was in the clubhouse, anyone was liable to show up—even Leo (The Lip) Durocher, his former manager and lifelong friend. On this day, Leo was in town for a card show. "Man," Mays said with his high-pitched laugh, "make sure you get your money. Don't do nothing for free!" Putting on a New York uniform always seemed to bring out the Say-Hey Kid. "I've given my life to this game, and I wouldn't change a thing," he said. "I'm happy, man. I'm happy."

He may have been Le Grande Orange in Montreal, but Mets fans loved Rusty Staub, too. They flocked to his restaurant, Rusty's, to chow down on barbecued baby-back ribs. Although Rusty's closed in 1991, his admirers can still enjoy its more upscale replacement, Rusty Staub's on Fifth Avenue. His 23-year career was something to be savored, too, all 2,716 hits and 292 home runs. Mets fans will always remember the record-tying eight consecutive pinch-hits, and the playoff game in 1973 when he nearly ran through the right-field wall to catch a ball hit by Cincinnati's Dan Driessen. "I would never trade in the memories and good times I had in New York for anything," he said on Rusty Staub Day at Shea in 1986.

BOB MURPHY

A popular and beloved broadcaster, Bob Murphy has entertained and enthralled Mets fans since the team's inception. An "Original Met," he joined up with Lindsey Nelson and Ralph Kiner in 1962 to entertain the radio and television audience with wit and information. The trio broadcast together until 1979, when Nelson left to work for the San Francisco Giants. Beginning in 1982, Murphy broadcast exclusively on radio, while Kiner handled televison. A veteran of over 6,000 games and still going strong, Murphy has called the team's three pennants, rating Game 6 of the 1986 playoffs as the best game he has ever seen. Rewarded for many years of outstanding service, Murphy was inducted into the Baseball Hall of Fame on July 31, 1994.

Pete Flynn, an Original Met, has been head groundskeeper at Shea since 1974. A native of Ireland, Flynn, 54, moved to New York in 1961 and joined the Mets shortly thereafter.

GEORGE WHITFIELD

Known as the Grandfather of the Vendors, George Whitfield (above) has been selling scorecards at Shea since the stadium opened. The good-natured Whitfield, 87, grew up near Ebbets Field in Brooklyn, and used to sell newspapers outside the park. Later, in the 1920s, he began to hawk scorecards, ice cream and soda to Dodger fans. He's worked for Harry M. Stevens, Inc., the New York-based concessionaire, for 54 years. "I always did good for myself," says Whitfield, who can often be found at the Gate D entrance.

Harry M. Stevens practically invented ballpark food. He opened his first concession stand at the Polo Grounds more than 90 years ago, and quickly came up with the idea to put a sausage in a bun. Today, Stevens' company is responsible for cooking and selling thousands of hot dogs at each Mets game, along with knishes, chicken wings, deli sandwiches, ice cream bars and other delights.

The Famous San Diego Chicken pays a visit to Shea.

Violinist Itzhak Perlman performs the National Anthem for the fans at Shea on opening day.

Young fans at the ball park dream of the future. From the dugout, Drew Saberhagen (at right) intently watches his father practice.

THE NEW BREED

Clockwise from top left, the next generation of Mets: McReynolds, Miller, Strawberry, Dykstra and Carter.

Empty, Shea Stadium isn't much to look at. Full, it's a vibrant, colorful, exciting place to be. Fortunately, over the years, it's been full a lot more than it's been empty.

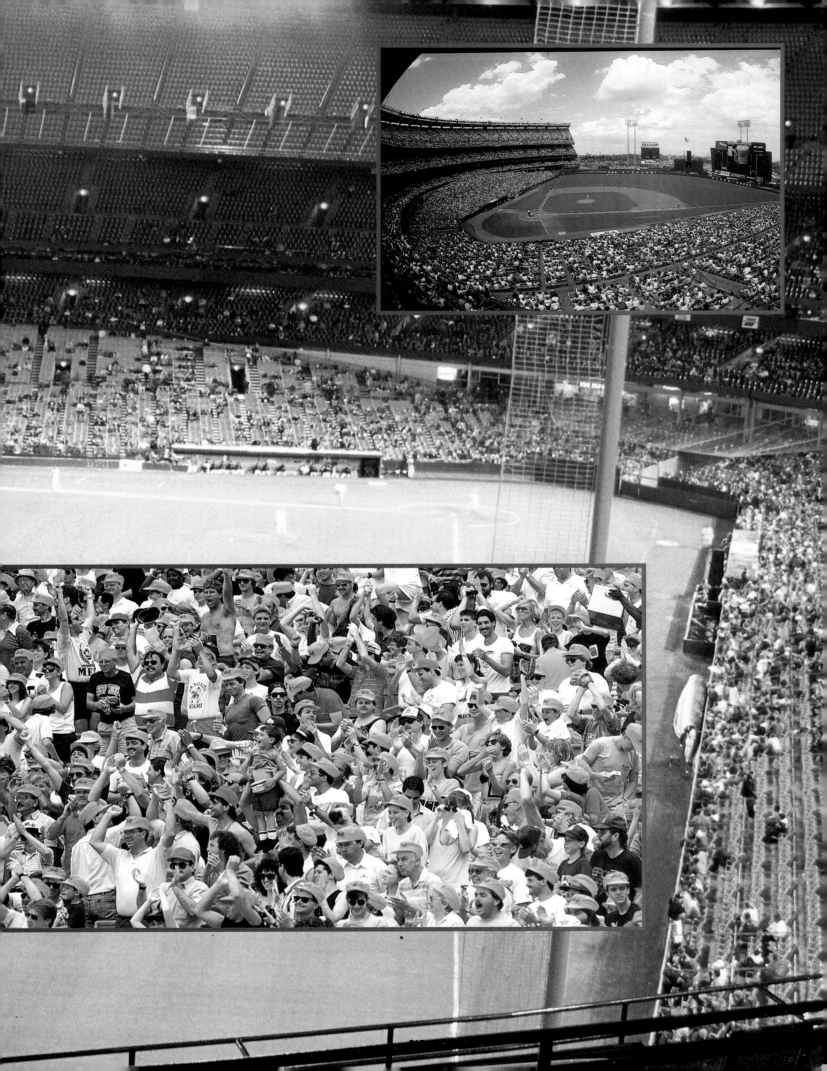

GATE B   FIELD & LOGE LEVELS   GATE B

Fireworks
and baseball make
a magical pair
on a beautiful
New York
summer night.

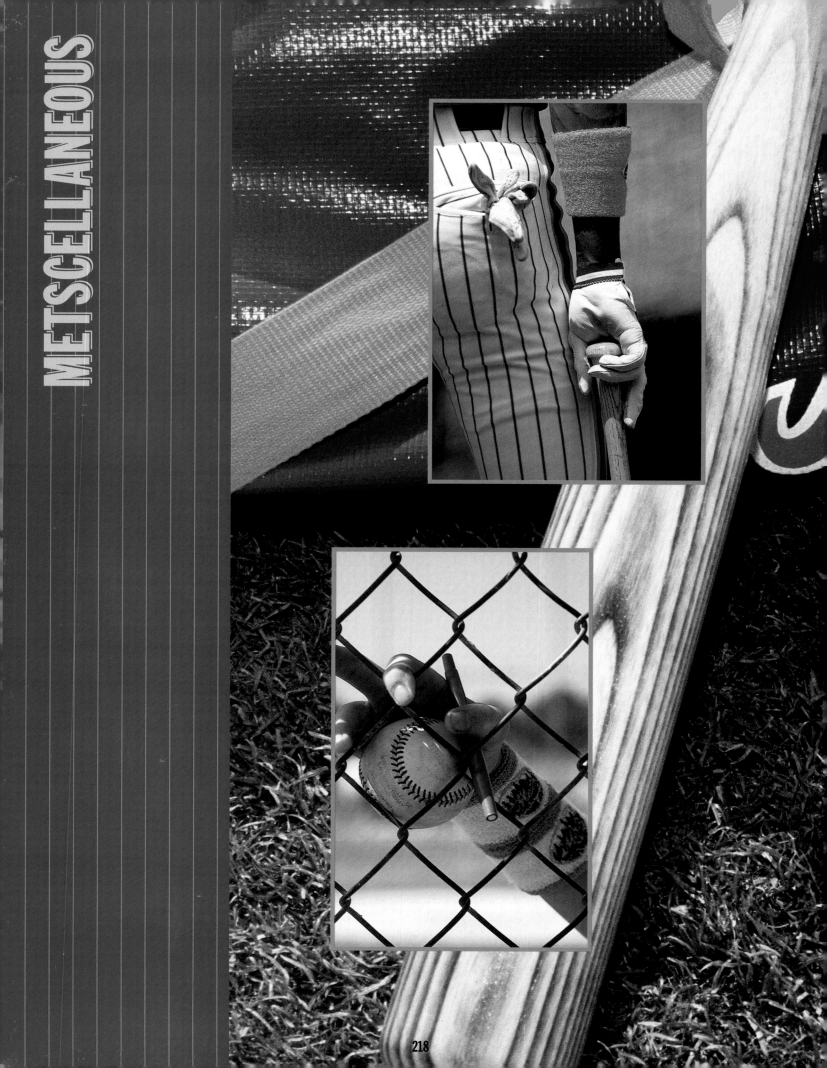

METSCELLANEOUS

Although major
league baseball
often must be
viewed from a
distance, baseball
itself is best viewed
close-up. Batting
practice is the best
time to approach the
backstop, near
enough to watch
the rituals and
listen to the cadence
of the game.

Mookie Wilson and his stepson, Preston, who later became the Mets' No. 1 pick in the 1992 draft. A third baseman, Preston is climbing the organizational ladder, paying his dues in the minor leagues. Meanwhile, Mookie, who retired in '91 after three years with Toronto, has returned to the Mets as a community outreach representative and minor league instructor.
Baseball is indeed a family affair.

The Mets All-Time Roster as of July 15, 1994
(Participated in at least one game)

AASE, Don 1989 (RHP)
AGEE, Tommie 1968-72 (OF)
AGUILERA, Rick 1985-89 (RHP)
AKER, Jack 1974 (RHP)
ALLEN, Neil 1979-83 (RHP)
ALMON, Bill 1980, 87 (IF)
ALOMAR, Sandy 1967 (SS)
ALOU, Jesus 1975 (OF)
ALTMAN, George 1964 (OF)
ALVARADO, Luis 1977 (2B)
ANDERSON, Craig 1962-64 (RHP)
ANDERSON, Rick 1986 (RHP)
APODACA, Bob 1973-79 (RHP)
ARRIGO, Gerry 1966 (LHP)
ASHBURN, Richie 1962 (OF)
ASHFORD, Tucker 1983 (IF)
ASPROMONTE, Bob 1971 (IF)
AYALA, Benny 1974-76 (OF)
BACKMAN, Wally 1980-88 (IF)
BAEZ, Kevin 1990, 92-93 (IF)

BROGNA, Rico 1994- (1B)
BROOKS, Hubie 1980-84, 91 (IF-OF)
BROSS, Terry 1991 (RHP)
BROWN, Kevin 1990 (RHP)
BROWN, Leon 1976 (OF)
BRUHERT, Mike 1978 (RHP)
BUCHEK, Jerry 1967-68 (2B)
BURKE, Tim 1991-92 (RHP)
BURNITZ, Jeromy 1993- (OF)
BURRIGHT, Larry 1963-64 (IF)
BURRIS, Ray 1979-80 (RHP)
CANDELARIA, John 1987 (LHP)
CANGELOSI, John 1994 (OF)
CANNIZZARO, Chris 1962-65 (C)
CAPRA, Buzz 1971-73 (RHP)
CARDENAL, Jose 1979-80 (OF)
CARDWELL, Don 1967-70 (RHP)
CARMEL, Duke 1963 (1B)
CARR, Chuck 1990-91 (OF)
CARREON, Mark 1987-91 (OF)

DILLON, Steve 1963-64 (LHP)
DONNELS, Chris 1991-92 (IF)
DOZIER, D.J. 1992 (OF)
DRAKE, Sammy 1962 (2B)
DRAPER, Mike 1993 (RHP)
DWYER, Jim 1976 (OF)
DYER, Duffy 1968-74 (C)
DYKSTRA, Len 1985-89 (OF)
EDENS, Tom 1987 (RHP)
EILERS, Dave 1965-66 (RHP)
ELLIOT, Larry 1964, 66 (OF)
ELLIS, Dock 1979 (RHP)
ELSTER, Kevin 1986-92 (SS)
ESPINOSA, Nino 1974-78 (RHP)
ESTRADA, Chuck 1967 (RHP)
ESTRADA, Francisco 1971 (C)
FALCONE, Pete 1979 82 (LHP)
FERNANDEZ, Chico 1963 (SS)
FERNANDEZ, Sid 1984-93 (LHP)
FERNANDEZ, Tony 1993 (IF)
FERRER, Sergio 1978-79 (IF)
FILER, Tom 1992 (RHP)
FISHER, Jack 1964-67 (RHP)
FITZGERALD, Mike 1983-84 (C)
FITZMAURICE, Shaun 1966 (OF)
FLORES, Gil 1978-79 (OF)
FLYNN, Doug 1977-81 (IF)
FOLI, Tim 1970-71, 78-79 (IF)
FOLKERS, Rich 1970 (LHP)
FOSS, Larry 1962 (RHP)
FOSTER, George 1982-86 (OF)
FOSTER, Leo 1976-77 (IF)
FOY, Joe 1970 (3B)
FRANCO, John 1990-(LHP)
FREGOSI, Jim 1972-73 (3B)
FRIEND, Bob 1966 (RHP)
FRISELLA, Danny 1967-72 (RHP)
GAFF, Brent 1982-84 (RHP)
GALLAGHER, Bob 1975 (OF)
GALLAGHER, Dave 1992-93 (OF)
GARDENHIRE, Ron 1981-85 (SS)
GARDNER, Jeff 1991 (IF)
GARDNER, Rob 1965-66 (LHP)
GARDNER, Wes 1984-85 (RHP)
GARRETT, Wayne 1969-76 (3B)
GASPAR, Rod 1969-70 (OF)
GENTRY, Gary 1969-72 (RHP)
GIBBONS, John 1984, 86-87 (C)
GIBSON, Bob 1987 (RHP)
GIBSON, Paul 1992-93 (LHP)
GILES, Brian 1981-83 (IF)
GINSBERG, Joe 1962 (C)
GLYNN, Ed 1979-80 (LHP)
GONDER, Jesse 1963-65 (C)
GOODEN, Dwight 1984 (RHP)
GOOSSEN, Greg 1965-68 (C)
GORMAN, Tom 1982-85 (LHP)
GOSGER, Jim 1969, 73-74 (OF)
GOZZO, Mauro 1993- (RHP)
GRAHAM, Bill 1967 (RHP)
GRAHAM, Wayne 1964 (3B)
GREER, Kenny 1993 (RHP)
GREEN, Dallas 1966 (RHP)
GREEN, Pumpsie 1963 (3B)
GRIEVE, Tom 1978 (OF)
GROTE, Jerry 1966-77 (C)
GRZENDA, Joe 1967 (LHP)
GUETTERMAN, Lee 1992 (LHP)
GUNDERSON, Eric 1994- (LHP)
HAHN, Don 1971-74 (OF)
HALL, Tom 1975-76 (LHP)
HAMILTON, Jack 1966-67 (RHP)
HAMPTON, Ike 1974 (C)
HARE, Shawn 1994- (OF)
HARKNESS, Tim 1963-64 (1B)
HARRELSON, Bud 1965-77 (SS)
HARRIS, Greg 1981 (RHP)
HARTS, Greg 1973 (PH)
HASSLER, Andy 1979 (LHP)
HAUSMAN, Tom 1978-82 (RHP)
HEARN, Ed 1986 (C)
HEBNER, Richie 1979 (3B)
HEEP, Danny 1983-86 (OF)
HEIDEMANN, Jack 1975-76 (IF)
HEISE, Bob 1967-69 (IF)
HENDERSON, Ken 1978 (OF)
HENDERSON, Steve 1977-80 (OF)
HENDLEY, Bob 1967 (LHP)
HENNIGAN, Phil 1973 (RHP)
HEPLER, Bill 1966 (LHP)
HERBEL, Ron 1970 (RHP)
HERNANDEZ, Keith 1983-89 (IB)
HERNANDEZ, Manny 1989 (RHP)
HERR, Tom 1990-91 (2B)
HERRSCHER, Rick 1962 (IF)
HICKMAN, Jim 1962-66 (OF)
HICKS, Joe 1963 (OF)
HILLER, Chuck 1965-67 (IF)
HILLMAN, Dave 1962 (RHP)

BOB GIBSON and JOE TORRE

HILLMAN, Eric 1992- (LHP)
HINSLEY, Jerry 1964, 67 (RHP)
HODGES, Gil 1962-63 (1B)
HODGES, Ron 1973-84 (C)
HOLMAN, Scott 1980, 82-83 (RHP)
HOOK, Jay 1962-64 (RHP)
HOLMAN, Scott 1980, 82-83 (RHP)
HOUSIE, Wayne 1993 (OF)
HOWARD, Mike 1981-83 (OF)
HOWELL, Pat 1992 (OF)
HUDSON, Jesse 1969 (LHP)
HUGHES, Keith 1990 (OF)
HUNDLEY, Todd 1990- (C)
HUNT, Ron 1963-66 (2B)
HUNTER, Willard 1962, 64 (LHP)
HURDLE, Clint 1983, 85, 87 (C)
HURST, Jonathan 1994- (RHP)
HUSKEY, Butch 1993 (IF)
INNIS, Jeff 1987-93 (RHP)
JACKSON, Al 1962-65, 68-69 (LHP)
JACKSON, Darrin 1993 (OF)
JACKSON, Roy Lee 1977 80 (RHP)
JACOME, Jason 1994- (LHP)

JEFFERIES, Gregg 1987-91 (IF)
JEFFERSON, Stanley 1986 (OF)
JELIC, Chris 1990 (IF)
JOHNSON, Bob D. 1969 (RHP)
JOHNSON, Bob W. 1967 (IF)
JOHNSON, Howard 1985-93 (IF-OF)
JONES, Barry 1992 (RHP)
JONES, Bobby 1993 (RHP)
JONES, Cleon 1963, 65-75 (OF)
JONES, Randy 1981-82 (LHP)
JONES, Ross 1984 (SS)
JONES, Sherman 1962 (RHP)
JORGENSEN, Mike 68, 70-71, 80-83 (1B)
KANEHL, Rod 1962-64 (IF)
KAISER, Jeff 1993 (LHP)
KENT, Jeff 1992- (IF)
KINGMAN, Dave 1975-77, 81-83 (1B)
KLAUS, Bobby 1964-65 (IF)
KLEVEN, Jay 1976 (C)
KLIMCHOCK, Lou 1966 (PH)
KNIGHT, Ray 1984-86 (3B)
KOBEL, Kevin 1978-80 (LHP)

BAILOR, Bob 1981-83 (IF)
BALDWIN, Billy 1976 (OF)
BALDWIN, Rick 1975-77 (RHP)
BARNES, Lute 1972-73 (IF)
BASS, Kevin 1992 (OF)
BAUTA, Ed 1963-64 (RHP)
BEANE, Billy 1984-85 (OF)
BEARNARTH, Larry 1963-66 (RHP)
BEATTY, Blaine 1989-91 (LHP)
BEAUCHAMP, Jim 1972-73 (1B)
BELL, Gus 1962 (OF)
BENNETT, Dennis 1967 (LHP)
BENTON, Butch 1978-80 (C)
BERENGUER, Juan 1978-80 (RHP)
BERENYI, Bruce 1984-86 (RHP)
BERNARD, Dwight 1978-79 (RHP)
BERRA, Yogi 1965 (C)
BETHKE, Jim 1965 (RHP)
BIRKBECK, Mike 1992 (RHP)
BISHOP, Mike 1983 (C)
BLOCKER, Terry 1985 (OF)
BOCHY, Bruce 1982 (C)
BOGAR, Tim (IF) 1993-
BOISCLAIR, Bruce 1974,1976-79 (OF)
BOITANO, Dan 1981 (RHP)
BOMBACK, Mark 1980 (RHP)
BONILLA, Bobby 1992-(IF-OF)
BOSCH, Don 1967-68 (OF)
BOSTON, Daryl 1990-92 (OF)
BOSWELL, Ken 1967-74 (2B)
BOUCHEE, Ed 1962 (1B)
BOWA, Larry 1985 (SS)
BOYER, Ken 1966-67 (3B)
BRADLEY, Mark 1983 (OF)
BRESSOUD, Ed 1966 (SS)

CARTER, Gary 1985-89 (C)
CASTILLO, Tony 1991 (LHP)
CERONE, Rick 1991 (C)
CHACON, Elio 1962 (IF)
CHANCE, Dean 1970 (RHP)
CHAPMAN, Kelvin 1979,1984-85 (IF)
CHARLES, Ed 1967-69 (3B)
CHILES, Rich 1973 (OF)
CHITI, Harry 1962 (C)
CHRISTENSEN, John 1984-85 (OF)
CHRISTOPHER, Joe 1962-65 (OF)
CISCO, Galen 1962-65 (RHP)
CLENDENON, Donn 1969-71 (1B)
CLINES, Gene 1975 (OF)
COLEMAN, Clarence 1962-63, 66 (C)
COLEMAN, Vince 1991-93 (OF)
COLLINS, Kevin 1965, 67-69 (IF)
CONE, David 1987-92 (RHP)
CONNORS, Bill 1967-68 (RHP)
COOK, Cliff 1962-63 (OF)
CORCORAN, Tim 1986 (IF)
CORNEJO, Mardie 1978 (RHP)
COWAN, Billy 1965 (OF)
CRAIG, Roger 1962-63 (RHP)
CRAM, Jerry 1974-75 (RHP)
CUBBAGE, Mike 1981 (IF)
DARLING, Ron 1983-91 (RHP)
DAVIAULT, Ray 1962 (RHP)
DAVIS, Tommy 1967 (OF)
DeMERIT, John 1962 (OF)
DENEHY, Bill 1967 (RHP)
DEWEY, Mark 1992 (RHP)
DIAZ, Carlos 1982-83 (LHP)
DIAZ, Mario 1990 (IF)
DiLAURO, Jack 1969 (LHP)

1981 OFFICIAL SCORE BOOK

DAVE and RUSTY RETURN

$1.00 INCL. TAX

KOLB, Gary 1965 (OF)
KOONCE, Cal 1967-70 (RHP)
KOOSMAN, Jerry 1967-78 (LHP)
KRANEPOOL, Ed 1962-79 (1B)
KROLL, Gary 1964-65 (RHP)
LABINE, Clem 1962 (RHP)
LAMABE, Jack 1967 (RHP)
LANDRITH, Hobie 1962 (C)
LANDRUM, Ced 1993 (OF)
LARY, Frank 1964-65 (RHP)
LATHAM, Bill 1985 (LHP)
LEACH, Terry 1981-82, 85-89 (RHP)
LEARY, Tim 1981, 83-34 (RHP)
LEWIS, Johnny 1965-67 (OF)
LIDDELL, Dave 1990 (C)
LINDEMAN, Jim 1994- (OF)
LINTON, Doug 1994- (RHP)
LINZ, Phil 1967-68 (2B)
LOCKE, Ron 1964 (LHP)
LOCKWOOD, Skip 1975-79 (RHP)
LOLICH, Mickey 1976 (LHP)
LOMBARDI, Phil 1989-90 (C)

LUPLOW, Al 1966-67 (OF)
LYNCH, Ed 1980-86 (RHP)
LYONS, Barry 1986-90 (C)
MACHADO, Julio 1989-90 (RHP)
MacKENZIE, Ken 1962-63 (LHP)
MADDOX, Elliot 1978-80 (OF)
MADDUX, Mike 1993- (RHP)
MAGADAN, Dave 1986-92 (1B,3B)
MANGUAL, Pepe 1976-77 (OF)
MANKOWSKI, Phil 1980, 82 (3B)
MANTILLA, Felix 1962 (IF)
MANZANILLO, Josias 1993- (RHP)
MARSHALL, Dave 1970-72 (OF)
MARSHALL, Jim 1962 (1B)
MARSHALL, Mike 1981 (RHP)
MARSHALL, Mike A. 1990 (OF)
MARTIN, J.C. 1968-69 (C)
MARTIN, Jerry 1984 (OF)
MARTINEZ, Teddy 1970-74 (IF)
MASON, Roger 1994- (RHP)
MATLACK, Jon 1971-77 (LHP)
MAY, Jerry 1973 (C)

METS vs CUBS SEPTEMBER 21 & 22

$2.00

Scho Field of Dreams

MAYS, Willie 1972-73 (OF)
MAZZILLI, Lee 1976-81, 86-89 (OF)
McANDREW, Jim 1968-73 (RHP)
McCLURE, Bob 1988 (LHP)
McCRAY, Rodney 1992 (OF)
McDANIEL, Terry 1991 (OF)
McDOWELL, Roger 1985-89 (RHP)
McGRAW, Tug 1965-67, 69-74 (LHP)
McKNIGHT, Jeff 1989,1992- (OF)
McMILLAN, Roy 1964-66 (IF)
McREYNOLDS, Kevin 1987-91, 94- (OF)
MEDICH, George 1977 (RHP)
MERCADO, Orlando 1990 (C)
METZGER, Butch 1978 (RHP)
MILLAN, Felix 1973-77 (2B)
MILLER, Bob G. 1962 (LHP)
MILLER, Bob L. 1962, 73-74 (RHP)
MILLER, Dyar 1980-81 (RHP)
MILLER, Keith 1987-91 (IF-OF)
MILLER, Larry 1965-66 (LHP)
MILLIGAN, Randy 1987 (OF)
MILNER, John 1971-77 (1B-OF)
MITCHELL, John 1986-89 (RHP)
MITCHELL, Kevin 1984 86 (OF)
MIZELL, Wilmer 1962 (LHP)
MOFORD, Herb 1962 (RHP)
MONTANEZ, Willie 1978-79 (1B)
MOOCK, Joe 1967 (3B)
MOORE, Tommy 1972-73 (RHP)
MOORHEAD, Bob 1962, 65 (RHP)
MORALES, Jerry 1980 (OF)
MORAN, Al 1963-64 (IF)
MORENO, Jose 1980 (IF)
MURPHY, Bill 1966 (OF)
MURRAY, Dale 1978-79 (RHP)
MURRAY, Eddie 1992-93 (IF)
MUSGRAVES, Dennis 1965 (RHP)
MUSSELMAN, Jeff 1989-90 (LHP)
MYERS, Randy 1985-89(LHP)
MYRICK, Bob 1976-78 (LHP)
NAVARRO, Tito 1993 (IF)
NAPOLEON, Dan 1965-66 (OF)
NEAL, Charlie 1962-63 (IF)
NIEMANN, Randy 1985-86 (LHP)
NOBOA, Junior 1992 (IF)
NOLAN, Joe 1972 (C)
NORMAN, Dan 1977-80 (OF)
NUNEZ, Edwin 1988 (RHP)
O'BRIEN, Charlie 1990-93 (C)
OJEDA, Bob 1986-90 (LHP)
O'MALLEY, Tom 1989-90 (IF)
OQUENDO, Jose 1983-84 (SS)
OROSCO, Jesse 1979, 81-87 (LHP)
ORSULAK, Joe 1993 (OF)
ORTIZ, Junior 1981-83 (C)
OSTROSSER, Brian 1973 (SS)
OTIS, Amos 1967, 69 (OF)
OWNBEY, Rick 1982-83 (RHP)
PACELLA, John 1977, 79-80 (RHP)
PACIOREK, Tom 1985 (C)
PARKER, Harry 1973-75 (RHP)
PARKER, Rick 1994- (OF)
PARSONS, Tom 1964-65 (RHP)
PECOTA, Bill 1992 (IF)
PEDRIQUE, Al 1987 (IF)
PEMBERTON, Brock 1974-75 (1B)
PENA, Alejandro 1990-91 (RHP)
PFEIL, Bob 1969 (3B)
PHILLIPS, Mike 1975-77 (IF)
PIERSALL, Jim 1963 (OF)
PIGNATANO, Joe 1962 (C)
POWELL, Grover 1963 (LHP)
PUIG, Rich 1974 (IF)
PULEO, Charlie 1981-82 (RHP)
RAJSICH, Gary 1982-83 (OF)
RAMIREZ, Mario 1980 (IF)
RANDLE, Len 1977-78 (IF)
RANDOLPH, Willie 1992 (2B)
RAUCH, Bob 1972 (RHP)
REARDON, Jeff 1979-81 (RHP)
REED, Darren 1990 (OF)
REMLINGER, Mike 1994- (LHP)
RENIFF, Hal 1967 (RHP)
REYNOLDS, Ronn 1982-83, 85 (C)
REYNOLDS, Tom 1967 (OF)
RIBANT, Dennis 1964-66 (RHP)
RICHARDSON, Gordon 1965-66 (LHP)
RIVERA, Luis 1994- (SS)
ROBERTS, Dave 1981 (LHP)
ROHR, Les 1967-69 (LHP)
ROSADO, Luis 1977, 80 (1B)
ROSE, Don 1971 (RHP)
ROWE, Don 1963 (LHP)
RUSTECK, Dick 1966 (LHP)
RYAN, Nolan 1966, 68-71 (RHP)
SABERHAGEN, Bret 1992- (RHP)
SADECKI, Ray 1970-74, 77 (LHP)
SAMBITO, Joe 1985 (LHP)
SAMUEL, Amado 1964 (OF)

SAMUEL, Juan 1989 (OF)
SANDERS, Ken 1975-76 (RHP)
SANTANA, Rafael 1984 87 (SS)
SASSER, Mackey 1988-92 (C)
SAUNDERS, Doug 1993 (IF)
SAUVEUR, Rich 1991 (LHP)
SCARCE, Mac 1975 (LHP)
SCHAFFER, Jim 1965 (C)
SCHATZEDER, Dan 1990 (LHP)
SCHIRALDI, Calvin 1984-85 (RHP)
SCHMELZ, Al 1967 (RHP)
SCHNECK, Dave 1972-74 (OF)
SCHOFIELD, Dick 1992 (SS)
SCHOUREK, Pete 1991- 93 (LHP)
SCHREIBER, Ted 1963 (IF)
SCHULZE, Don 1987 (RHP)
SCOTT, Mike 1979-82 (RHP)
SEARAGE, Ray 1981 (LHP)
SEAVER, Tom 1967-77, 83 (RHP)
SEGUI, David 1994- (1B)
SELMA, Dick 1965-68 (RHP)
SEMINARA, Frank 1994- (RHP)
SHAMSKY, Art 1968-71 (OF)
SHAW, Bob 1966-67 (RHP)

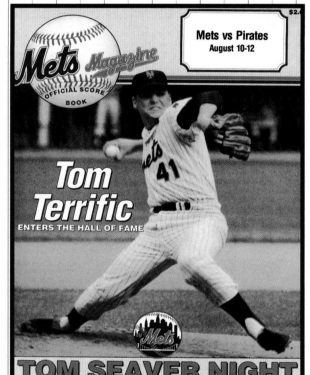

Mets vs Pirates August 10-12

$2.00

OFFICIAL SCORE BOOK

Tom Terrific

ENTERS THE HALL OF FAME

TOM SEAVER NIGHT

SHAW, Don 1967-68 (LHP)
SHERRY, Norm 1963 (C)
SHIPLEY, Craig 1989 (IF)
SHIRLEY, Bart 1967 (2B)
SHORT, Bill 1968 (LHP)
SIEBERT, Paul 1977-78 (LHP)
SIMONS, Doug 1991 (LHP)
SINGLETON, Ken 1970-71 (OF)
SISK, Doug 1982-87 (RHP)
SMITH, Bobby Gene 1962 (OF)
SMITH, Charley 1964-65 (3B)
SMITH, Dick 1963-64 (OF)
SMITH, Pete 1994- (RHP)
SNIDER, Duke 1963 (OF)
SPAHN, Warren 1965 (LHP)
SPRINGER, Steve 1992 (IF)
STAHL, Larry 1967-68 (OF)
STAIGER, Roy 1975-77 (3B)
STALLARD, Tracy 1963-64 (RHP)
STANTON, Leroy 1970-71 (OF)
STAUB, Rusty 1972-75, 81-85 (OF)
STEARNS, John 1975-84 (C)
STEPHENSON, John 1964-66 (C)
STERLING, Randy 1974 (RHP)
STINNETT, Kelly 1994- (C)
STONE, George 1973-76 (LHP)
STRAWBERRY, Darryl 1983-90 (OF)
STROHMAYER, John 1973-74 (RHP)
STROM, Brent 1972 (LHP)
STUART, Dick 1966 (1B)
STURDIVANT, Tom 1964 (RHP)
SUDAKIS, Bill 1972 (C)
SULLIVAN, John 1967 (C)
SUTHERLAND, Darrell 1964-66 (RHP)
SWAN, Craig 1973-84 (RHP)

SWEET, Rick 1982 (C)
SWOBODA, Ron 1965-70 (OF)
TABLER, Pat 1990 (OF)
TANANA, Frank 1993 (LHP)
TAPANI, Kevin 1989 (RHP)
TATE, Randy 1975 (RHP)
TAVERAS, Frank 1979-81 (SS)
TAYLOR, Bob 1964-67 (C)
TAYLOR, Chuck 1972 (RHP)
TAYLOR, Ron 1967-71 (RHP)
TAYLOR, Sammy 1962 63 (C)
TELGHEDER, Dave 1993- (RHP)
TEMPLETON, Garry 1991 (IF)
TERRELL, Walt 1982-84 (RHP)
TERRY, Ralph 1966-67 (RHP)
TEUFEL, Tim 1986-91 (IF)
THEODORE, George 1973-74 (OF)
THOMAS, Frank 1962-64 (OF)
THOMPSON, Ryan 1992- (OF)
THORNTON, Lou 1989-90 (OF)
THRONEBERRY, Marv 1962-63 (1B)
TIDROW, Dick 1984 (RHP)
TILLMAN, Rusty 1982 (OF)
TODD, Jackson 1977 (RHP)

TORRE, Joe 1975-77 (IF)
TORREZ, Mike 1983-84 (RHP)
TORVE, Kelvin 1990-91 (1B)
TREVINO, Alex 1978-81, 90 (C)
TWITCHELL, Wayne 1979 (RHP)
VAIL, Mike 1975-77 (OF)
VALENTINE, Bobby 1977-78 (2B)
VALENTINE, Ellis 1981-82 (OF)
VALERA, Julio 1990-91 (RHP)
VERYZER, Tom 1982 (SS)
VINA, Fernando 1994- (IF)
VIOLA, Frank 1989-91 (LHP)
VITKO, Joe 1992 (RHP)
VIZCAINO, Jose 1994- (SS)
WAKEFIELD, Bill 1964 (RHP)
WALKER, Chico 1992-93 (IF-OF)
WALTER, Gene 1987 (LHP)
WASHINGTON, Claudell 1980 (OF)
WEBB, Hank 1972-76 (RHP)
WEIS, Al 1968-71 (IF)
WEST, Dave 1988-89 (LHP)
WESTON, Mickey 1993 (RHP)
WHITEHURST, Wally 1989-92 (RHP)
WILLEY, Carl 1963-65 (RHP)
WILLHITE, Nick 1967 (LHP)
WILLIAMS, Charlie 1971 (RHP)
WILSON, Mookie 1980-89 (OF)
WINNINGHAM, Herm 1984 (OF)
WOODLING, Gene 1962 (OF)
WYNNE, Billy 1967 (RHP)
YOUNG, Anthony 1991-93 (RHP)
YOUNGBLOOD, Joel 1977-82 (OF)
ZACHRY, Pat 1977-82 (RHP)
ZIMMER, Don 1962 (3B)